Pigeon Shooting

Pigeon Shooting

John Gray

The Crowood Press

First published in 1988 by
The Crowood Press Ltd
Ramsbury, Marlborough,
Wiltshire SN8 2HR

This impression 1994

British Library Cataloguing-in-Publication Data

Gray, John
    Pigeon shooting.
    1. Great Britain. Woodpigeons. Shooting – Amateurs' manuals
    I. Title
    799.2′4865

    ISBN 1 85223 084 3

Acknowledgements

Photographs by Nick Turley and *Sporting Gun*.
Line illustrations by Janet Sparrow.

My sincere thanks are due to:
Diane Farnden, Nick Turley, Maurice Richardson, *Sporting Gun*,
Alan Graham, John Storry, Julia Smith, Mike George, Gillian Evitt
and Cecil Jacobs. Also to my father, for instilling in me a love of
shooting, and all those farmers upon whose land I have pursued
this marvellous sport. And, last but not least, the woodies.

Typeset by Avonset, Midsomer Norton, Bath
Printed and bound in Great Britain by BPC Hazell Books Ltd,
A member of The British Printing Company Ltd

Dedication

This book is dedicated to my wife, Ilma, who exemplifies the patience shown by all shooting wives for their erstwhile menfolk.

Contents

Foreword by Robin Scott   9

Introduction   11

1 Agricultural Pest and Sportsman's Quarry   15

2 Equipment   21

3 Decoys   37

4 Setting Up   65

5 Oil Seed Rape – The Big Challenge   80

6 Main Crops   87

7 Roost Shooting and Flighting   100

8 Memorable Moments   109

Conclusion   120

Recipes   122

A Pigeon Shooter's Country Code   124

Useful Addresses   125

Index   126

Foreword

Every sportsman has his favourite quarry. Some wax lyrical about driven pheasants; others, a hard-won goose prised from a bitter dawn on some god-forsaken salting in deepest January. This book, though, puts the woodpigeon firmly on top. And quite rightly too in my view – no other species can touch it for the sheer variety of sport and downright excitement it affords to thousands of people every month of the year. It truly is a bird for all seasons.

Against such odds, you might wonder how on earth the woodpigeon ever manages to survive, let alone thrive, in our country-side. Yet it does and very nicely too, thank you. Modern agriculture has a lot to do with its proliferation of course but so too, I suspect, does the hit-or-miss approach adopted by many sportsmen when it comes to tackling the legions of pigeon which inhabit the woods and hedgerows of Britain.

This book, I fancy, will help redress the balance somewhat. However, I think it worth giving the so-called 'numbers game' a mention. Putting together big bags of pigeon is a satisfying experience of course, but we don't all live in parts of the country where such obliging concentrations exist. In fact I would say that in some areas a sportsman who manages to finish the day with 15 or 20 birds can count himself every bit as skilled as the pigeon shooter with access to much greener pastures.

Pigeon shooting is many things to many men but one thing it isn't is competitive. And heaven forbid that it should ever become so. This book will appeal to all thinking pigeon shooters. For the minority who are obsessed with bag size and kills-to-cartridge ratios, it should become compulsory reading. It could just rekindle the enjoyment that they have lost on the way . . . both for a day in the open air and for a bird that deserves their healthiest regard.

Robin Scott

Introduction

The average pigeon shooter is not a professional pest controller or crop protector, but a sportsman gunner. He and his kind represent a relatively small section of Britain's 58 million population but even so there may well be as many as 300,000 people who shoot pigeons, ranging from the specialist decoyer to the less dedicated casual pigeon 'potter'.

Let me say immediately that I am not concerned in any way with professional crop protection and pigeon control as a business. I am interested in pigeon shooting purely as a leisure activity. This sport enables those of us with fairly limited means to engage in shooting live quarry – and to be perfectly honest, if it was not for the pigeon then the opportunity to do just that would be extremely limited for many of us.

I do not view this sport as a humble activity which is merely the control by shooting of a creature viewed by many almost as vermin. The woodpigeon is a worthy quarry and it is extremely fortuitous that we

The average pigeon shooter is not a professional pest controller or crop protector, but a sportsman gunner.

have at our disposal in this country a relatively large population of such a sporting bird, although I recognise that not everyone will agree with me, particularly farmers.

The woodpigeon (*Columba palumbus*) is also called the ring-dove because of its collar of white feathers. It has, however, a number of regional names. When I was a boy in Herefordshire, we referred to them as quists. In most shooting magazines and amongst most shooters, this sporting bird is referred to as the 'woody'.

The woodpigeon ranges over much of Britain but it concentrates in its greatest numbers in the arable areas. At certain times of the year, pigeons congregate in large numbers on particular crops, oil seed rape being the primary example. When this happens the pigeon is naturally perceived by farmers as an economic threat and hereby hangs the admission sign for the pigeon shooter's access to the land.

Pest

In Great Britain, because the woodpigeon is identified as an agricultural pest, there is no 'close' season for the bird and they may be shot all the year round. It is a matter of individual conscience whether the pigeon shooter decides to continue shooting during the height of the breeding season, which covers the months of June, July and, particularly, August; August being the peak. Incidentally, fertile eggs have been found in every month of the year.

My own view is that pigeon numbers are little threatened by the amount of summertime shooting which actually takes place. There is also scant, if any, evidence to suggest that many nest-bound 'squabs' are condemned to starvation as a result of both parents, which share feeding responsibilities, being shot. The greatest factor which deters many shooters in high summer is often the weather. I have had my own share of sweaty, 'fly-blown' days, shooting over

laid corn, and for me they bear no comparison with the clear, bright, windy days of spring or autumn.

When I was young the rabbit was farming's 'public enemy' number one. I was most impressed as a youngster in the 1950s to read somewhere that five rabbits ate as much as one sheep. I can well recall how wide strips around fields of cereals would be eaten bare by rabbits, so I can accept that this creature did in fact pose a formidable economic threat to farmers. I am prepared to stick my neck out and say that I am not convinced that woodpigeons impose the same sort of threat. I think it is important to state this, since I believe it would be disastrous if pigeons were seen as a problem of the same magnitude as rabbits once were – remember it was felt necessary to control rabbit numbers by the introduction of myxomatosis.

When you empty the bulging crop sack of a bird which has fed well, it is always impressive to see how much an individual bird is able to consume. I believe, however, that calculations designed to show how much tonnage, and consequently how much in money terms of farm crops is lost per year to pigeons, are purely academic. The amount of grain lost on an individual farm is hardly likely to have a ruinous effect on the farmer. In my opinion the pigeon becomes a pest and an economic threat in specific instances; for example, when a significant number of birds are allowed unrestricted feeding on a particular crop to the point of its despoilation as a viable proposition. I am thinking particularly of a field of oil seed rape which suffers severe pigeon damage, possibly coinciding with a prolonged frost, and is thereby so hard-hit that it becomes necessary to plough it up and sow an alternative crop. This situation causes a cash loss to the farmer with the extra costs incurred in further cultivation, seed, time and labour. It is of course the worry that this type of tangible damage may occur, rather than the more intangible

The pigeon shooter appreciates the quiet places where he may be alone with his thoughts.

losses caused by pigeons feeding on laid corn for instance, which prompts a farmer to take protective measures.

Crop Protection

Farmers employ a number of gadgets to attempt to disturb pigeons feeding on valuable cash crops. These measures range from gas-operated banger guns, revolving luminous bird scarers driven by wind, to the latest sonic devices which make a loud 'whiffling' sound. Many farmers I know will patrol their rape field by Landrover early in the morning to move on any feeding flock.

It has been my experience that pigeons appear to get used to most, if not all, of these methods quite quickly and for the most part they are ineffective on the large acreages which comprise many modern fields. I cannot count how many times I have witnessed a flock of pigeon feeding in close proximity to a banger gun and merely lift in the air when the gun fires and resettle within a short distance, to carry on feeding. These devices are hardly likely to succeed when almost every arable farmer is employing them with the hope of moving his unwelcome avian visitors on to his neighbours' land. It is against this background that the pigeon shooter makes his entrance as the more effective of the deterrents, since he not only protects crops by his presence on the land but he is also seen to control pigeon numbers by shooting.

In the years that I have been shooting pigeons I have always been mindful of the need to report back to any farmer who has given me permission to shoot. Nothing consolidates your continuing access to a particular farm more than giving a farmer the occasional view of a substantial boot-load of slain pigeon. I have found that farmers thus impressed are men who will welcome you back time and time again, because if you are seen to be an effective slayer of pigeon, then you are perceived to be a worthy guardian of the farmer's livelihood.

Appeal

Although all pigeon shooters, including me, live in the hope of regularly making a good-sized bag of birds, the size of the bag is in fact irrelevant to the true sportsman's enjoyment of pigeon shooting as a pastime. The pleasure which pigeon shooting generates does not derive from the shooting and killing of a living creature, as field sports opposers would have the otherwise uncommitted or disinterested citizen believe. The field-craft involved in bringing that creature within effective range of your shotgun and then the final test of marksmanship certainly has much to do with the sport's appeal, but this is not the whole story by any means. There is a great need in our modern society to escape for a while from the mass of humanity which encroaches inevitably upon our individual living space. The meadows and woods offer an escape to solitude for the field sportsman or woman. The sights and sounds you witness form the true essence of pleasure and memory. A pigeon shooter is not a rural vandal gratuitously slaughtering wildlife, nor is he solely a crop protector. Rather he is a lover of the countryside and its creatures, appreciating the everchanging moods of weather and sky and the quiet places, where he may be alone with his thoughts whilst exercising the perfectly natural hunting urge which still exists in modern, largely urbanised, man.

1 Agricultural Pest and Sportsman's Quarry

Acquiring a Shooting Territory

The first consideration of those who are relative novices at the sport, is usually how to acquire some land upon which to shoot, so I will deal, therefore, at this early stage, with the important aspect of seeking permission. I have personally been successful in building up a shooting territory, but there is no magic formula involved, just time, common sense, a little knowledge of agriculture and an attention to simple social courtesies.

I am not enamoured with the thought that some people deem it necessary to buy pigeon shooting. This sport should be, and is, for the dedicated enthusiast, a do-it-yourself business all the way from obtaining permission to shoot to the actual finding and decoying of the quarry. We are dealing with a wild bird which knows no territorial boundary and will change its food or feeding location at will or as circumstances dictate. It is a true hunting sport and the shooter must go where the birds are. Advertisements offering pigeon shooting for sale are in fact selling access to the land. Very few people could guarantee a successful day's sport in the way that a day at pheasants can be sold and relatively guaranteed to produce a given bag.

So, if buying pigeon shooting is generally inadvisable, the answer is of course to 'get on your bike', or more accurately, into your vehicle. I realise that for town dwellers a bit more travelling may be incurred than for their country cousins but after all our country is not *that* big and distances are not vast. A steady ride round the countryside in your area, noting its general character and physical features, will prove revealing. Building up a mental picture of your territory in this way is very important because it is vital to know the type of crops being grown and the potential for sport locally. Where there is a predominance of grassland little opportunity for regular decoying may exist, whereas a pattern of mixed arable farming is more likely to be sustaining a substantial local pigeon population. In this respect those of us who live in central, southern and eastern England and certain areas of lowland Scotland, have a distinct advantage over our fellow sportsmen from other parts of the realm. Shooting men from both the North and the South-West have frequently told me that their opportunity to shoot tends to be both seasonal and sporadic. To those in this situation I am not unsympathetic, nor unmindful that I am fortunate to live in the arable Midlands, an area which holds a reasonable year-round pigeon population.

Knowing an area and the crops grown in it will give an indication of its potential for sport. Likewise, scouting excursions, armed with a pair of binoculars, will eventually result in pigeon being spotted, either feeding on a field or flighting to a location which it should be possible to pinpoint. All experienced shooters are agreed that reconnaissance and time spent just patiently watching is vital.

Reconnaissance and time spent patiently watching is vital.

Seeking Permission

Once a likely spot has been located, then permission must be sought. I follow a simple set of rules from here on which have been effective for me; so much so that I would claim rarely to have been refused when seeking permission.

First of all I do not like telephoning a farmer, since a disembodied voice will not tell him sufficient about the man with whom he is dealing. I always call in person as the farmer needs to base his judgement of whether to let you shoot or not on appearance as well as what you sound like. It is also vital to know the man's name. This may seem obvious, but not everyone pays this heed even though it is so important.

Avoiding likely mealtimes is advisable, but sometimes easier said than done. If you find on calling that a meal has been interrupted then apologise and offer to call again. It may be that you will be asked to do just that, or, as frequently happens, you may be asked to state your business there and then.

It is always possible quickly and succinctly to state your case. Beating about the bush in your approach is best avoided, so be direct and to the point. The information you give should be your name, where you have seen the birds feeding and that you would like to decoy them. I always explain that decoying entails shooting from a fixed spot and will not involve traipsing all over the farm. It pays, I feel, to add that no mess will be left and that all empty cartridge cases will be picked up. It is useful to tell the farmer that you will report back to let him know the result of your activities, for then he is reassured that he has tabs on what you are doing. If your case is delivered in an open, friendly, civil manner, your request will very likely be positively received.

It is worth adding that driving steadily down driveways or into farmyards is sensible. Speed or flying gravel suggests aggression or recklessness and these are attitudes which you definitely do not wish to convey. Furthermore, arriving in a camouflage suit or clothed in other obvious shooting gear may appear presumptuous, and being over-dressed creates an equally bad impression. Appearances are important so striking a happy medium pays; I suppose being smartly casual is about right.

I do not want to give the impression that it is always plain sailing. Some farmers will inevitably say no and there are a variety of reasons for this. Perhaps an approach has been too blunt and lacking in finesse. Someone else may have been badly let down by other pigeon shooters and therefore have decided to ban them all. Sometimes a farmer who is a keen shooter himself fears his gamebirds will be disturbed, whilst yet another may feel that to give permission to shoot, even on one occasion, is yielding a right to access which he is generally uneasy about giving. All these reasons have to be respected of course. Put yourself in the farmer's position and think how readily you might permit a total stranger to shoot on your land. I know how territorial I am and what my answer might well be – that is why I regard the pigeon shooting I have gained as an earned privilege, to be respected and safeguarded.

There are times when a farmer cannot give permission because the shooting is let to a tenant or the farm is part of an estate and the will of the keeper prevails. When this is the case, if the farmer wishes his crop to be protected he will often seek approval from the appropriate authority for pigeon shooters to be allowed to operate. If it is left to you as an individual to seek permission from a third party then the style of approach described earlier is still valid.

Follow the Rules

When you have finally gained access to shoot pigeons where you have indicated their presence to be, it is sensible to follow a few simple rules. Stick to that field and go nowhere else on the farm without further leave to do so. It is also inadvisable to take either a friend or dog unless you have been told that this is permissible. Unruly, untrained dogs are always best left at home anyway, being no asset whatsoever for the man who shoots from a hide.

There will be times when game birds present themselves but you must *not* give in to temptation to take game when you have been admitted on trust to shoot pigeons. It is not only unprincipled but foolish. It may appear that no one is around but the countryside has 'eyes' and your misdemeanour may well not go unwitnessed. Transgressions will not only spoil your chances for building up shooting locally but possibly ruin it for others as well.

All in all, a pigeon shooter should leave little evidence of his presence on a field, save for a scattering of pigeon feathers and perhaps a patch of flattened grass by the hedgeside where the hide was located. Empty cases and general litter should all be taken home as you have pledged, so that neither farmer nor gamekeeper is caused offence by an avoidable, unsightly mess.

The first man to give you permission to shoot is, in a way, the key to being successful in your subsequent enquiries with other local farmers. If you establish your credentials on one farm there can surely be no harm in a bit of name-dropping on another.

Personal Beginnings

When I first moved to my present house, I left my previous shooting territory behind me. It was a matter of some frustration that I did not have access to a single acre in my new home area upon which to shoot. One

A whisper of wings and woodpigeons overhead.

day I happened to be in conversation with an acquaintance who said he was very much involved with clay shooting. I replied that my interest in shooting lay in pursuing live quarry, particularly pigeon, but that since I had recently moved to the area, nothing as yet was forthcoming. The result of this conversation what that on the following Saturday I was invited to a roost shoot which the local clay shooting club were organising.

It was the last Saturday in January and we assembled close to the keeper's cottage. Old hands were directed to areas of woodland with which they were familiar. Newcomers had precise directions given to them as to where they should go. I was one of a group of three who were personally taken to a section of woodland near the big house and placed in position by the keeper.

A whispering silence had descended over the wood as I explored my immediate location. A solitary robin piped somewhere near and from far off in a distant meadow the melancholy cawing of a carrion crow carried harshly, echoing on the stillness of a winter's afternoon. Here and there rhododendron bushes were growing on the woodland floor and I managed to find one whose all-embracing branches lent a ready-made hide overlooking a relatively clear area of woodland.

The watery afternoon sun had only just dipped before a whispering of wings heralded the first arrivals, as a small group of woodpigeon flashed overhead. My first two hurried shots had one bird down, and so my first step into a new pigeon shooting territory was taken.

The roost shoot ended, if I remember

correctly, with a total bag of 90, 21 having fallen to my own gun. I made it my business to speak to the keeper, explaining my desire to obtain pigeon shooting locally. The information gained was that there was a farmer in my own village who might help in my quest. The next day I introduced myself to this farmer who explained that a local estate was looking for a responsible person to decoy pigeon, over rape. I was given the manager's name and permission to say who had sent me. Needless to say, within minutes I was introducing myself to the farm manager, and, luckily, permission was readily granted.

It was a cold day with snow lying in patches. A bitter wind heralding more snow blew from the north west. I set out my small pattern of six birds, victims of Saturday's roost shoot, and settled into the natural hide I had made in the hedge. An hour and a half's shooting produced 28 birds before the first snow flurries turned into a steady fall and all activity ceased.

I remember that time with pleasure and gratitude, for it was the beginning of my pigeon shooting activity locally. All the other shooting I have obtained, which I estimate to be access to around fourteen thousand acres, has grown from that beginning.

Perseverance Pays

I would advise a hopeful shooter to persevere when seeking permission. My father and I had been getting good sport off a farm which lay on a hillside, backed with woodland. We arrived late on a Saturday morning close to Easter, only to find that the drilling we had anticipated as being a real pigeon draw had in fact nothing whatsoever on it. I glassed the area and noticed that far across the valley, behind a large country house, there was a long narrow field of drilling running parallel to a brook. I could also see the birds were working this field in some quantity. It was a simple matter to make enquiries in the village as to the owner of the land. I discovered that he indeed lived in the large house overlooking the countryside I had been scouting.

It was with a little trepidation that I rang the doorbell. No one answered for quite a while and then echoing footsteps approached the door. It swung open, and a tailcoated gentleman in pin-striped trousers confronted me – the butler. I stated my case: there were pigeons, I wished to shoot them, and would it be possible to speak to Mr. P. The request was met cordially, but firmly – no, his employer was resting and besides, the shooting on the estate was the privilege of the men who worked there. The chances of shooting would be nil.

My anticipation seemed to have disappeared, when I suddenly hit a moment's inspiration. I enquired if there was a farm manager. The answer was in the affirmative, so armed eventually with his name and address I set off again on my quest for permission. I found the manager's house and rang the bell, again with a trepidation born of anticipation and fear of failing in my request. The door was answered by a friendly-looking chap who listened patiently to my request. 'Yes of course have a go at the blighters,' was the reply. 'We only drilled that field two days ago, so you should have some luck if they are at it already.'

That evening, dad and I found it really hard work to get off that field, as 90 birds, plus equipment, are no mean weight to carry. My first task was to return to the manager to let him see the result of my afternoon's work. Today I am aware that this estate is my most valued and productive section of land. It holds pigeon for year-round decoying, and its woodlands, to which I have unrestricted access, are marvellous for roost shooting. I think back to how easily I might have been put off by that butler and his desire to leave his employer undisturbed. I reiterate, if you want pigeon shooting, *persevere*.

A decoy pattern being laid out over drilling.

Clubs

Apart from the individual approach, you can also gain pigeon shooting through the auspices of a shooting club. Pigeon shooting clubs and wild fowling associations with pigeon shooting interests, exist throughout the UK. These range from well organised, properly constituted groups of perhaps fifty members or more, to small three or four man affairs. It is quite usual for a club to be affiliated to the BASC, so an individual member gains not only pigeon shooting but the benefits derived from being affiliated to the wider association as well.

Pigeon shooting clubs have advantages and disadvantages. Often there is a waiting list for membership and it may well be a case of stepping into a dead man's shoes for an individual to gain entry. Being a member of a club means you may well have to take the rough with the smooth and at times go where the field officer directs you to go, rather than where your own inclination as a hunter might otherwise take you. I am sure, however, that for most shooting club members the benefits of belonging to an organised group outweigh any of the slight disadvantages. For the busy man with a living to earn and time short for reconnaissance and obtaining permission to shoot, it must be a godsend to have someone prepare the ground for him.

One shooting club I visited in East Anglia offering a crop protection service to farmers, was a marvellously organised body which fulfilled a social function as well as a shooting one and members seemed well satisfied that they were getting value for their annual subscription.

In the years to come, as shooting grows in popularity, legislation and accountability to authority may well increase and it could be that the shooting club will be the way forward into the next century for the pigeon shooter. It is my earnest hope, however that there will always be a place for the individual, who, like me, values his independence to seek, organise and follow his sport as he desires.

2 Equipment

Years ago when I was interested in coarse fishing, there were always those chaps who appeared on the river bank laden down with gear. I could only afford one rod and a limited amount of tackle so I viewed the other fellows with a certain amount of awe. Whether their surfeit of equipment made them any more adept at the catching of fish or not I do no know, but they certainly looked professional. In this sport of pigeon shooting it is possible to obtain and carry a great deal of equipment. New innovations are constantly being produced and were we to acquire everything, then certainly one, if not two Sherpas would be required to help carry our gear on to a field.

I do recognise that for many people innovating or purchasing the latest piece of kit has a certain attraction. Indeed, my own father, bless him, is a gadget man. I am afraid I am not. I list the equipment I consider necessary for pigeon shooting under three headings: essential, useful to the point of being essential, and useful but not essential.

Guns and Cartridges

The most essential item of equipment is obviously the shotgun. Whether it is an over-under or side-by-side, twelve bore or

Whether the shotgun has barrels which are over-under or side-by-side, like this one, is immaterial.

twenty bore, full, choke, half, quarter or improved cylinder barrels in the first instance is totally irrelevant as far as I am concerned. When I started shooting I did not have the indulgence of choice. The shotgun which was available was the one for the job. I recognise that we now live in a more affluent age (for most people), and that choosing a gun is a matter of great concern for many aspiring shooters. My advice is to seek guidance from a good gunsmith who will counsel you as to the most suitable tool for the job.

I see no merit for either over-under or side-by-side configuration and believe it to be a matter of personal choice. I shot with a 30 inch barrelled 'Charles Boswell' side-by-side for many years until it went into honourable retirement. I now use a 26 inch barrelled over-under. The change took a little bit of getting used to but I think my shooting is now better than ever. I made the point to a well-known shooting coach that perhaps, as I am a fairly large man, a longer barrelled gun might have suited me better. He replied, 'John, if you are shooting well, for heaven's sake stick with it.' I believe this to be good advice. A gun which fits you, feels right, comes up well and with which you have been successful, is one with which to build a long term partnership. We pigeon shooters should not become too wound up about our guns. Competitive clay shooters may require absolute, spot-on performance. I would argue that if a pigeon shooter's gun is performing satisfactorily and he is generally happy with it, it does not matter if his performance could be marginally improved or not. An extra bird per box of cartridges is an irrelevance to me, whereas to the competitive clay shooter it may be the difference between success and failure. I will reiterate that our sport is not an entirely quantifiable activity in terms of birds shot, although we do owe it to our quarry to either miss completely or kill cleanly.

My own gun is bored a quarter and half choke. Experts on these matters will often

quote improved cylinder and quarter choke with 28 inch barrels as being the optimum length. Perhaps for someone who has not been shooting all that long or who has not formed a strong preference either way, this may indeed be a useful configuration to aim for when acquiring a new or replacement gun. Even so, good professional advice will be invaluable.

When I first acquired my present gun I wondered if the single selective trigger would pose a problem. I am pleased to say that it has not given me the slightest trouble. I can select the barrel I wish to use more quickly than choosing the front or rear trigger on my old gun since I have incorporated the selection of the barrel to be fired and the pushing off of the safety into one movement. The single trigger action also makes for some very fast snap shooting over decoys.

I have so far made no reference to the use of semi-automatic or pump action shotguns. These are quite popular as pigeon guns but I have little experience of them and cannot say that they would figure as being my choice of weapon. My feelings are, I admit, based purely on limited usage of this type of gun. Pump action guns seem very unwieldy to me and the semi-automatics I have fired appeared to make a weird, offputting noise as the ejector mechanism clanked into action. I do not think that the average shot is likely to increase his bag size in any way by using an automatic as opposed to a more conventional gun, although I am ready to concede that many experienced and skilled shooters use them satisfactorily.

The average shooter can become totally baffled by the technicalities and merits of this or that gun, which so many experts tend to bombard us all with. I know I am soon lost when discussions become too technical. One fact I do know is that a long barrelled, tightly choked gun will generally throw too close a pattern of shot for the efficient and consistent killing of pigeon

A 26 inch barrelled over-under shotgun, a handy weapon in the restricted space of a hide.

over decoys at the usual range of perhaps 15–40 yards, with the optimum somewhere in between. Too tight a pattern may result in two things; the average or less than average shot may find that a higher percentage of misses results from the tighter pattern area of shot thrown, and birds shot at closer distances may well be smashed up as a consequence of being hit by high density of shot.

Cartridge Loads

Pattern is determined not only by barrel length and choke but also by the cartridge used. Modern plastic shot cups tend to produce tighter patterns so the size of shot is also quite important. This is an area of some controversy and discussion, even amongst experienced pigeon shooters. When I was younger I tended to use $1\frac{1}{8}$oz of five shot. Over the years, this was modified to $1\frac{1}{8}$oz of six shot. After some years of pigeon shooting I settled upon $1\frac{1}{16}$oz of seven shot as being the most suitable for my needs. My shooting partner asked me a few years ago why I had never considered using 1oz loads. My answer was that it was probably psychological and although I wanted a lightish load considering my light game gun, I felt that 1oz was probably too light. I have an open mind and eventually decided to try 1oz loads of seven shot. Suffice it to say I found this loading to be quite as efficient for shooting decoyed or roosting pigeon as anything I had ever used. I am not going to be accused of pushing any particular cartridge or loading for pigeon shooting, I am just stating how my personal preference gradually evolved, over quite a few years at this sport. I know shooters who use heavily loaded trap cartridges for pigeon. If they are happy with this and find they do the job, so what! There are no mandatory rules to say that this or that cartridge must be used. Pigeon shooting can result in the discharge of quite a number of cartridges in a short while. A sweet, light, load through a relatively light gun is a godsend. If my 1oz loads did not kill effectively and consistently at the range I am shooting, that is up to a maximum of 45 yards, I would not use them.

I mentioned earlier the plastic shot cup which is incorporated in modern cartridges. This is a matter of some concern for field shooters. One pigeon shooter I know was appalled to find that following a session decoying birds which were coming to oak trees to glean acorns in parkland, the pasture was absolutely covered with plastic shot cups. No farmer is going to take a sympathetic stance if he loses stock which have consumed any of these. Until a plastic which has a rapid biodegradable quality is devised, it may be advisable for pigeon shooters operating where stock will be feeding to use a more traditional cartridge incorporating fibre wadding.

Gun Security

Anyone who is in possession of a lethal weapon is under the obligation to keep it secure and safe, either from opportunist thieves or the inquisitive hands of children. It may well be, before this book is all that old, that keeping shotguns in secure purpose-built security cabinets will be a prerequisite to the granting of a shotgun certificate.

Many shooters abhor the notion that gun security should ever be made into a legislative issue. I personally cannot see what is wrong with keeping a weapon securely — after all, owning a gun represents quite an investment in financial terms. I have had a purpose-built gun safe for years. My own gun safe is not particularly good-looking, but that matters little for it does not occupy a prominent position in my home. Gun security, however, does not have to sacrifice pleasing looks to functional usefulness and there are many good-looking cabinets on the market which, if one is prepared to pay the price, are quite elegant enough to dress even the most salubrious drawing room. Gun security makes sense and I would urge anyone owning a shotgun to invest in a police approved cabinet.

You may well wonder what all this has got to do with pigeon shooting. I take the view that we cannot separate our sport from wider sociological considerations. The armed siege, the once-in-a-lifetime murderous aberration, concern us all, for they inevitably threaten our right to legitimately own and use guns for sporting purposes. So anything we as responsible gun owners can do to make sure our weapons do not fall into the wrong hands must eventually help in some small way to safeguard our sport.

Dispatch of Wounded Birds

It is the duty of all sportsmen to minimise the chances of wounding the quarry. Shooting speculatively at long range targets will inevitably produce a higher percentage of wounded birds, so first and foremost do not shoot at birds which you do not have a more than sporting chance of killing. Secondly, it is incumbent upon all shooters of living creatures to ensure that their own personal marksmanship is as good as it possibly can be, even if it means going clay shooting to gain sufficient experience.

Despite all our best efforts, it is inevitable that some birds will be wounded, or 'winged' as I call it. It is our duty to dispatch these birds as quickly, painlessly and cleanly as possible. It surprises me how inept otherwise skilled field sportsmen can be,

Gun security is essential, but function need not be sacrificed to good looks. A fine gun cabinet from Clay Shooters Supplies Ltd.

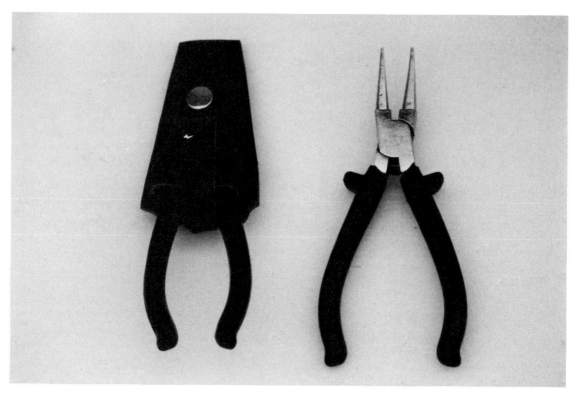

Humane equipment for dispatching all kinds of birds. 'Game Killers' from Shooting Developments.

when confronted with the necessity of dispatching wounded pigeon. I have dispatched many thousands of turkeys and other poultry in my time and am very adept at breaking the neck of birds without pulling off the head with its messy consequences. Most novices are *not*.

What can the pigeon shooter do to overcome this problem? Do not swing the bird by the neck as some so-called experienced shooters do; this may dispatch the bird, but it is an altogether impractical way of dealing with the problem. Similarly, some shooters use a weighted stick called a priest, with which to give the stricken creature a sharp rap to the head – this is effective, but clumsy!

There are purpose-built dispatchers on the market which are basically a type of pliers which can be employed to cleanly break the neck of a wounded bird without mess. This is an unsavoury subject I know and one best avoided by good shooting, but it has to be faced and provision made to deal humanely with wounded birds.

Binoculars

Once you have your gun and choice of cartridges then you have the only really essential equipment necessary to shoot pigeons. This is a fact since sufficient birds can often be shot for decoys by being in the right place, and no decoys are necessary anyway for roost shooting. Hides can be made from natural materials and lofting gear is certainly not essential. Of course no one dreams of pursuing pigeon shooting with a view to creating regular sport without the

Hides can be made from natural materials.

aid of ancillary equipment in excess of the bare essentials of gun and cartridges. Reconnaissance, that is using your eyes, counts so much towards the ultimate success you enjoy at this sport. It is natural therefore that extending your range of vision is extremely important. Money invested in a good pair of binoculars is well spent. Nowadays there are rubberised models which are designed to withstand the hard use that field sportsmen are likely to give them. A good choice would be 10×50. A higher magnification than $\times 10$ will be hard to hold steady without a stand. There was a time when I did not possess a pair of binoculars, but to be truthful, I wonder how I ever managed without any.

Net Hides and Poles

I have had opportunity to talk to many pigeon shooters at venues such as the Game Fair. It always surprises me to discover that there are still those who use extremely heavy, old fashioned, camouflage netting. The drawbacks of this kind of material are its weight, bulk and its tendency to absorb water when rained on, which makes it heavier still. Modern lightweight netting is, I feel, quite expensive, but two or three pieces will give the basis of a good hide and will barely add any weight or bulk to the pigeon shooter's load.

Whenever possible I like to use a hide made of natural materials, or at least be able to incorporate natural materials in my hide. The problem is that modern farms tend to be so tidy and well trimmed round the

27

Lightweight hide poles and camouflage netting can make hide construction quick and easy.

edges, that natural material is difficult to come by. This is where the net truly comes into its own. Nowadays manufacturers not only make them in the standard dark green colour but also there is a net currently available which is a light olive brown on one side and light green on the other. I have found this particular colouring ideal for use when shooting over laid cereals and also during the autumn when the background colours are tending towards buff, yellow and brown.

In conjunction with camouflage netting, I carry a set of lightweight poles which double not only as the support structure for the hide material but also as a set of lofting poles. The set I have was commercially produced and comes in a hessian carrying sack. They have proved to be almost indespensible. I can set up a good hide quickly and with no fuss with my nets and poles which enables me to quickly get down to shooting. It also means I am flexible and mobile when required.

Carrying the Bag

In the game pocket of my waxproof shooting coat, I keep three game carriers. These are made of nylon strapping with a long metal loop at each end into which you thread the pigeons' heads so that they may be carried, suspended by the neck. These carriers enable me to transport large numbers of pigeon relatively easily off the field. I consider this the only way to carry the bag as it distributes the weight more efficiently for the person doing the carrying. Years ago I used a sack and if this was pretty full it often presented a problem to get it across my shoulders. When the sack was really full, the encumbrance of other gear and gun slung round me, made it near impossible to get it up on to the shoulders at all.

The weight that pigeon shooters carry can be incredible at times, so I always try to keep my gear to a minimum. If you go out

to a field already laden down then it is that much more difficult if a good bag has been made, to make the return journey in one go. With my game carriers I can carry in excess of a hundred birds along with my other gear. It is always a slog, especially if the vehicle is a field or two away and the going is tough underfoot. I often speculate whether I will be able to cope with the physical aspect of this sport in, say, late middle age, without some assistance, because it can be so extremely physically demanding when a good shoot has been made.

Hearing Protection

When you consider that pigeon shooting may entail the firing of a large quantity of cartridges in a confined space, it is vital to think seriously about using some form of hearing protection. I shot for years without using any device for hearing protection but now I would not dream of a day's decoying without protecting myself in some way. I remember how sometimes after a good pigeon shoot over decoys, a headache would follow. Since protecting my hearing I now never experience that type of noise-induced pain.

Hearing loss, caused by long term exposure to gun-fire, usually creeps up on its victim, who is often unaware that he is suffering any damage whatsoever to his hearing. I expect that all of us who have shot for some time without hearing protection, have suffered a degree of hearing loss. One of the main symptoms of inner ear damage (for that is what is entailed) experienced by the shooter, will be that he suffers a whistling sensation which is always there in the background. When this occurs it means that a degree of permanent hearing loss has been sustained. I have such a noise in my left ear and suspect that it is the result of sharing a hide with someone else and suffering the noise of their muzzle blast.

Game carriers are indispensable for carrying large quantities of pigeon.

*Gathering the slain. Even a few birds are awkward to carry in a
sack, hence my preference for game carriers which distribute the
weight evenly and leave my hands free.*

30

Protecting your hearing is vital.

It is certainly sensible for the young starting their shooting careers, to get into the good habit of protecting their hearing from the beginning. Old hands have nothing to lose, indeed quite a lot to gain by following suit. I have to be truthful and say that there are occasions when I break my own rule and fail to use any form of ear protection. When waiting by a pond for duck or in the wood for roosting pigeon, hearing plays an important part. Often the light whistle of wings will be the only signal you have of the immediacy of your quarry. On all other occasions I protect my ears.

There are a number of devices which the shooter may employ, either as a single line of defence or when ear plugs are used in conjunction with the ear-muff type of hearing protector. I used to find the latter type incredibly irritating to use but have now got used to them and use this sort exclusively. Whatever the individual shooter chooses as his form of protection, it is, as in all things, a matter of personal preference. However, a wad of cotton wool pushed in the ears is, more or less, a waste of time.

Clay pigeon shooters have long realised the importance of wearing hearing protection. I would strongly advise pigeon shooters to take a leaf out of our clay busting colleagues' book and to do the same.

Modern technology is a wonderful thing and I have recently discovered that there are some new ear-muff protectors on the market which not only allow you to hear normally but may actually enhance your hearing. Now this is a truly significant innovation as far as the field shooter is concerned. I certainly intend to acquire a set of these protectors as soon as finances allow.

Seating

I think that there has been a real shortfall in the market-place of suitable seating for pigeon shooting. Nothing has really bettered the five gallon drum for comfort but it is a bulky, inconvenient, piece of kit and I long ago ceased to use one. Since then I have had a variety of seats, ranging from a neat folding job, guaranteed to hold up to six times my weight and which subsequently collapsed under me, to sawn down shooting sticks which were awkward to balance on.

I have now acquired a neat little fold-up seat which weighs a bare 3½lb and which comes in a sturdy camouflage material. It must prove to be a godsend for all hide shooters and is light and easy enough to carry into a roosting wood for use there as well as in a hide. It is important to be comfortable, considering the long waits invol-

A handy folding seat weighing a mere 3½lb, courtesy of Sporting Development.

ved in our sport. If you shoot from a sitting position or rise to take the shot, this seat should prove a winner either way.

Clothing

Clothing for pigeon shooting should be drab in colouring so that the wearer will blend with the background. There are various brands of clothing on the market produced in disrupted pattern material similar to military camouflage. Whether there is any general value in this type of colouring over a standard brown or green garment it is difficult to say, therefore it must boil down to a matter of personal choice.

Some pigeon shooters do not favour brown waxproof clothing because of its tendency to wear smooth and shiny. I wore a brown Barbour jacket for years and although it became very smooth I do not think it was ever responsible for spoiling a day's pigeon shooting.

In summer or on warmer spring days choice of clothing is straightforward – simply dress adequately to suit the conditions, and if it becomes too hot clothing can be removed. It is in the winter time when operating from a hide that the pigeon shooter can find himself inadequately attired. This may have dire consequences and be detrimental to health in the immediate and long term. It is all too easy in winter to underestimate the truly venomous nature of the weather.

A shooter, stationary in a hide, will be generating a fraction of the natural warmth which he would be producing if he was rough shooting. The chill factor of the wind, even though the actual air temperature is not all that low, can soon cause a pigeon shooter to feel very cold indeed.

I was shooting with a young farmer one day soon after Christmas. The ground had no visible frost on it yet it was rock hard. The sky had a look of snow, yet it never

Some shooters use a face veil to disguise the features.

the senses; it can, in extreme instances, kill. It is essential therefore to be well protected.

There are many good garments on the market made from material produced by modern technology. Some modern shooting coats are about half the weight of a traditional waxproof. Despite all this I feel that for the tough wear inflicted by pigeon shooting plus the ability to deter all weather, waxproof clothing still remains pretty well unbeatable. I have a beautiful shooting coat made in one of the new non-waxed materials but it is double the cost of a waxproof. Needless to say, it will never be subjected to the thorn-snagged, mud-bathing environment of a winter pigeon shooting hide.

A high proportion of warmth is lost through the top of the head so it makes sense to wear headcovering of some sort. A hat or cap has an added advantage besides preserving warmth, as the brim or peak shades the face and makes it less discernible by the quarry as belonging to a human. It is surprising how luminously a human face will shine over quite a long distance. Some shooters use face veils or pieces of net to disguise the features, particularly when roost shooting. I personally do not like peering through a piece of net. I used to favour a Balaclava helmet pulled up SAS-style. When I lost it I never replaced it and now just wear an orthodox hat or cap.

quite managed to precipitate and the wind was extremely strong with a cutting edge which stung our faces and sandpapered our lips. I was dressed, from the skin up, in several layers of clothing which were topped with a quilted waistcoat and finally one of Barbour's military-style waxproof suits. Despite all this it felt decidedly chilly, but bearable and certainly not sufficiently cold to drive me indoors. My companion, although slightly less adequately dressed, also had waxproofs on. He found that he could not stand the biting, numbing cold indefinitely and was finally driven home for hot soup and a chance to thaw out.

I feel that there is nothing macho in sticking it out when you find the cold unbearable. It can be dangerous to allow your body temperature to fall too low, too quickly. Cold drains the strength and dulls

The Dog

I expect that if my dog, Sam, had a human's sensitive ego, he would be slightly offended to realise that he was being categorised under the general heading of equipment, but since a dog can have an important role to play in our sport, this seems an opportune moment to itemise the function and merits of our canine companions in the context of pigeon shooting.

It is certainly not essential to have a dog and many pigeon shooters get by perfectly well without one. Having said that, I would argue that any sport which involves the shooting of live quarry is more humanely carried out when the sportsman is accompanied by a dog which is capable of retrieving wounded game.

In the first instance it is our duty as sportsmen to be as competent at shooting as our individual potentials as marksmen allow. Attempting to shoot at extended range is often speculative and should be avoided so as to minimise the risk of wounding. Despite our best efforts there will inevitably be times when a bird is 'winged'. The dogless shooter's first action must be to immediately retrieve the bird himself and to quickly dispatch it. The man who owns a good dog obviously has an efficient companion to undertake this labour for him.

A dog really comes into his own when a bird falls into thick cover, comes down over water, or towers away on the wind and drops half-way across the field. My own dog has saved my legs on every trip out. He often finds birds I have not marked down and probably pays for his own keep in retrieving these extra birds that I would otherwise have overlooked.

When you acquire a dog you take on a responsibility and commitment not unlike that of becoming a parent. Anyone who lives in restricted accommodation, or who feels a dog would be an inconvenience at holiday time, is advised to remain dogless. A gundog is only essential for the keen, committed shooter who is prepared to give it plenty of work. Too many people acquire a dog on impulse without considering the drawbacks and weighing up whether they have a real need of one.

It is also a matter of some consideration, if

An ideal breed for this sport, a Labrador retrieves a pigeon to hand.

The dog should retrieve only wounded birds, the ones which have fallen some way off, or those which have dropped in cover.

you decide to acquire a dog, as to which breed is best for a pigeon shooting companion. As far as I am concerned there is only one breed and that is a Labrador. A pigeon shooter has little need for an energetic, questing spaniel, or the specialised nature of one of the pointer types. Our requirement is for a biddable, patient retriever, which will sit quietly in a hide or roosting wood until instructed to work. In this respect the Labrador is unbeatable.

There are many good books about training gundogs and I would not be so presumptuous as to set myself up as an expert on the subject of training. I will, however, as the owner of a Labrador which performs well as a retriever of pigeon, venture one or two observations. Training a dog to be obedient, regardless of its final function as a gundog, is essential. When basic training in

obedience is established and training as a retriever begins, it is important not to introduce a young dog too quickly to pigeon. Pigeons are very loose feathered and a young, inexperienced dog, finding difficulty in getting a grip, will end up 'mouthing' the bird, which will lead either to a hard-mouthed dog or one reluctant to pick up pigeons.

I also consider it very important to have a dog which is steady to shot. It is no use having an animal which dashes out, demolishing your hide as it does so, each time you fire.

I think it is always a mistake to let your dog retrieve any and every bird you have down. Those birds which face down in front of the hide can be left until you go out to set them up as decoys. The dog should only be sent for wounded birds, the ones

35

A dog which is steady to shot is essential for shooting from a hide.

which have fallen some way off, or those which have dropped in cover.

A dog, like a shooter, matures and develops with experience. Most inadequate dogs are the result of inadequate training by inadequate owners. It is natural when you have a new pup that there should be a desire to get on and train it as a shooting companion as quickly as possible, but impatience can be disastrous. I know that I had to slow down when I first had Sam. I hope that I am not conveying the impression that my dog is of field trial standard, or a para-

gon of virtue, for he is not. He is an adequately trained, competent retriever of pigeon and not in the slightest bit hard-mouthed, yet he will relentlessly hunt down a moorhen and kill it if given half a chance. If he has the opportunity when travelling in the back of my estate car, he will also eat the heads off any pigeons he can reach. Nonetheless, I think the world of him and value the hours of pleasure we share together. Regardless of its practical function, a dog certainly adds another dimension of interest to your shooting.

3 Decoys

Artificial Birds

In this sport of pigeon shooting, it goes without saying that decoys, and the mechanical means of displaying decoys, are very important considerations. You will often hear criticism concerning the pulling power of commercially produced decoys. It is true that some have an inadequate colouring, or are rather too shiny; factors which may well, on occasion, actually deter approaching birds from coming into range, but we must be fair and say that despite this, artificial decoys do have a part to play under certain circumstances.

A shooter who engages in irregular bouts of decoying may well find a selection of artificial decoys convenient. A word of caution though – do not expect them to work under all conditions or at all times. Artificial decoys should be replaced in the pattern as birds are shot. Pulling the artificial birds in at least two at a time for every real bird set up is a useful guide. There is in the end no totally adequate substitute for real birds or decoys made from real birds but I will deal with this later.

There are many different types of artificial decoy on the market. They tend to vary in size, since some decoys are made slightly larger than life-size in the belief that they will appear more visible to the birds. Colour tends to vary as well, from make to make. You only have to lay several types of decoy side by side to see the wide range of differing blue and grey shades employed. Decoy types may be inflatable, semi-inflatable, full bodied, shell or a flat silhouette. They may also be presented in a head up or head down posture.

The main point to remember is that the best that any artificial decoys can achieve is a *resemblance* of the real thing, since neither mankind nor his modern technology has yet managed to emulate the creative touch of nature or if one believes in Him, the Almighty.

To underline the truth of this, hold a real bird against your favourite type of commercially produced decoy and ask yourself this, how effectively does the fake bird *really* copy the matt finish of the real thing? Is the colour *at all* like the real bird's? I shall be more than surprised if you have found a make which manages to match very closely these important features.

I have met shooters who swear by a particular type of decoy and would claim them deadly. This is of course first class and I am always delighted that anyone should have satisfactorily completed the quest for the perfect decoy, at least as far as their own requirements are concerned.

The perfect decoy must fulfil several criteria of course. It must have powers of attraction for living birds, which are as close to perfect as possible. It must also be light and easily transportable. In terms of lightness shell decoys obviously come to mind. Shells are very easy to transport and enough for a good pattern may weigh only around a pound. These decoys will wriggle attractively on their mounting sticks, adding that important simulation of life to the decoy pattern. Unfortunately, the drawback with them tends to be that they can appear unnaturally bright and shiny, factors which will often deter birds and make them reticent about coming into the pattern. A very strong wind can knock shell decoys about rather too much as well.

I took some shell decoys for a field trial

Light shell decoys from Sporting Developments.

A shell decoy set up on its peg.

Very light shell decoys on drilling.

one afternoon and used them to the exclusion of all others, including the birds I had shot. There was an initial reluctance on the part of the birds to come within shot but once the shoot got under way everything was fine and I went home with over eighty. I must confess, however, that on a similar afternoon when using shell decoys, the birds would not approach to a distance anywhere near within range before they turned off.

The type of commercially produced decoy in most people's possession is likely to be full bodied in design and either made of plastic or rubber. I have found that plastic decoys do tend to look very shiny, and they are also quite bulky. Although I am not generally a great fan of artificial decoys I do feel that their effectiveness is greatly enhanced when they are lofted on to trees. Plastic decoys are very useful for this and I have at times used them to good advantage in this way.

In the days when I was using rubber decoys, I found the Flexicoy type as effective as any. A friend of mine has some HH inflatables which he has found very effective, and they do indeed have a good reputation and are a well proven type.

Pigeons nowadays can become very wary and jumpy, particularly when they have received several baptisms of fire. They learn to mistrust decoys, especially if there is anything at all unnatural looking about the pattern. Not only do the birds acquire a reticence for coming into artificial decoys but, to be fair, there are times when they may show a reluctance about coming into a pattern consisting of real birds, especially if the decoys have been rained on and are covered with glistening drops of water.

On the whole though, real birds still work effectively and I shall deal later with various means of presenting them and indeed how, with a little time and trouble, you can make effective long-lasting shell decoys from real birds.

At this stage I would like to introduce

39

The author watches pigeon shooting equipment inventor and innovator, Maurice Richardson, at work.

you to a friend of mine, a pigeon shooter-cum-inventor and innovator of some note called Maurice Richardson who lives in East Anglia. Maurice, who is an engineer by calling, is a man of great ingenuity; he is also a possessor of great craft skills, a fact borne out by the magnificently turned wooden artefacts he produces in his spare time. He is a patient man who gives a problem, or an idea, much thought and gains great pleasure in coming up with an answer. I admire his contribution to the subject of pigeon decoys and their presentation and I am grateful to him for sharing his ideas with me. It is worth noting that a number of Maurice's ideas for presenting decoys are now commercially available from John Storry of East Anglian Shooting Products.

I am sure that all pigeon shooters would agree that adding movement to one's artificial flock can make the decoys all the more effective. If you watch a flock of birds feed-ing, especially on a dull day, what is most visible as the birds peck here and there, is the flashing of the white neck collars on the pigeons. Nature has given the pigeon this for the survival of the species, as it shows other pigeons where food has been found. If this pecking movement can be reproduced in decoys with little effort on the decoyer's part then this has to be an important innovation.

Maurice has come up with an adaptation made of a strip of spring steel, of the type found round packing cases or loads of bricks. This device is known as the Richardson Rocker and can be used with an artificial decoy or a shell made from a real bird. When a bird is mounted on the steel strip, which is then pushed into the ground, the wind will cause the decoy to bob in a very life-like manner.

I met a gentleman at a recent Game Fair who is devoted to a particular type of plastic

A full bodied plastic decoy and one which has been 'customised'.

(a)

(b)

A customised plastic decoy with a Richardson Rocker in place.

42

decoy. I showed him how this decoy could be modified by cutting away the bottom section, thereby turning the decoy into a shell. This reduces the weight and bulk to be carried but also allows for the decoy to be used with a Richardson Rocker. This customisation of a popular type of commercial decoy takes very little effort and yet enhances its attractiveness several times over. I have since received a letter from my Game Fair acquaintance in which he has indicated his delight for the manner in which his favourite decoys have been transformed.

Lofting

While we are on the subject of plastic decoys, I have used a device from John Storry, called an East Anglian Percher. This is basically a curved piece of wire with a counterweight at one end. The bird is mounted and then the device is hooked on a wire fence or the branch of a tree where it will ride through the strongest of winds.

I remember going in early summer to look at a field of wheat which had a few laid patches round the edge. Pigeon rose with a clatter from several of these fairly small areas at my approach. I placed the four plastic decoys I had with me on one of the laid areas but found that returning pigeon were very wary about approaching too close. I had three perchers with me so I mounted my decoys on these and placed them on some outside branches of a hedgerow tree close by one of the laid bits. The the other decoy I wedged in a forked branch. The decoys thus presented certainly appeared to pull the pigeons much more effectively. I had an added bonus in that over the hedge was a grass field and as pigeons were approaching the tree from that direction most of the birds I dropped fell on the grass where they were easily retrievable. I managed fifteen before rain stopped play.

I have tended to use lofted birds more frequently in recent years than in former times. It has become a necessary ploy particularly with the large acreages of oil seed rape we are now confronted with. Maurice Richardson has devised a frame for lofting dead birds which is well worth considering as useful equipment to carry. This frame consists of a cradle for holding the bird, with a spike for its head. There is a long counterweight 'tail' which can either be used as a handle for lofting by hand or slotted into a lofting pole for placing at a higher elevation. A curved portion under the cradle allows it to be hooked over a branch.

These same frames can be used for lifting a bird above a tall crop simply by sticking the tail end into the ground. As keeping the weight you must carry down to a minimum is such an important consideration, a piece of equipment like this, which fulfils two functions, is good news.

An East Anglian Percher from John Storrey.

A lofted, full-bodied plastic decoy using a Percher.

A lofting frame for a real bird.

A real bird mounted on the lofting frame.

Lofting by hand on an exposed outside branch.

A real bird lofted using Maurice Richardson's frames.

I do have one word of advice, though. When birds are lofted fairly high and a lofting pole is necessary to retrieve the bird and lofting frame, then it is necessary to put a plastic funnel in the end of the lofting pole. This allows the tail end of the frame to be guided easily into the end of the lofting pole, rather in the same way that two aircraft dock to refuel. Without a funnel it would be difficult, especially if the branches are swaying, to guide the end of the lofting pole to the end of the frame. These lofting frames are an invaluable piece of equipment and are now available commercially from the source I quoted earlier.

I took six dead birds as decoys to a field drilled with beans in April and, realising that several trees were proving very attractive to the pigeons, I employed my decoys as lofters using the lofting frames I have just described. I had a good shoot underway quite quickly and had shot at least a dozen pigeons before I made any attempt to make a pattern with them on the ground, the trees plus lofters proving a good enough draw.

It pays, when lofting birds on a tree with the hope of taking birds coming to them, *not* to build your hide directly under that tree. It can be difficult to shoot birds flying into a tree under which you are sitting. If cover is sparse and there are several attractive trees then I will sometimes break the rule and put my hide under one so that the trunk acts as a background to the hide. The decoys I of course put on one, or several, of the other trees as it will be easier to take birds coming into these.

A couple of winters ago I gained access to some rape fields which were set in some beautiful rolling countryside with an abundance of woodland and spinneys round and about. It was perfect pigeon holding territory and indeed, during February in particular, the pigeons were on the rape in great numbers. I found that my lofted birds were a godsend and by choosing well used trees I was fortunate to have several good shoots over a number of weeks.

On one occasion, a week after visiting these rape fields, I returned to a particularly favoured spot to find one of my lofted decoys still riding merrily away in one of the trees, despite a week of high winds. It can be so easy to overlook pieces of equipment in this way and you must discipline yourself into the habit of accounting for the items used.

Although you may think primarily of lofting as being the placing of decoys in trees, decoys which are raised only a few feet off the ground can in fact be made more visible. Real birds mounted on gate posts and fence posts can look very lifelike and are an attractive addition to the decoy pattern. Maurice has invented some wire frames which hold a real bird in a lifelike posture. This frame can be screwed into the top of a post and a bird mounted on it. The result is that a realistic effect of a live bird perched on a post is achieved. A variation of these frames can be used for mounting birds on the field so that they do not look as flat and dead as they might otherwise. I do not suggest, however, that it is necessary to mount all decoys this way, but it is a useful manner in which to present the first six dead birds with which you may start off the pattern.

Decoy Movement

I spoke earlier of the need to attain movement in the decoy pattern. To this end many pigeon shooters have taken to using a flapper. These are devices incorporating an artificial decoy which is presented with outstretched wings which can be flapped up

Mounting a real bird on a gate post using a purpose-made wire frame.

No, not a live pigeon but a decoy mounted using a special frame.

and down by pulling a string. Possibly the most popular type of flapper is a cradle for mounting a dead bird and incorporating some mechanical means of opening and closing the bird's wings. Locomotive power may come either from the decoyer by means of a length of line which must be pulled, or in some instances from a battery which works a small electric motor.

I mentioned in a previous section that I do not tend to employ a flapper cradle. This is not to say that I have never used one nor that I think that they are totally useless. The mistake some people make when using a flapper is to over-flap the bird's wings, which may scare pigeons which would have otherwise come into the decoy pattern.

Many shooters using a flapper also feel that they will be able to gain the attention of birds which are passing at a distance and which might not otherwise spot the decoys. I feel, as I said before, that the moving white collar flash of the pigeon is a long distance

signal and there are other efficient ways of emulating a feeding flock without recourse to a flapper. The Richardson Rocker previously mentioned is one of them.

All this does not mean a flapper is useless. Occasionally you will see pigeons, particularly high flying pigeons which are on course for a feeding place other than your chosen field, flick their wings at the decoy flock. What these passing pigeons are looking for is an answering flicker of wings from the ground. This is when the flapper should be used. All that is required is a swift opening and closing of the decoy bird's wings to emulate the answering feeding signal. Sometimes if a bird seems disinterested in the decoys a quick flick of the flapper's wings will entice it down. However, I must be honest and say that I have seen birds flick their wings at my decoys and although they have not received an answer, they have still committed themselves and come in.

As in all things, it is my opinion that if an

A good example of a pigeon flapper.

A flexible rod (aerial is perfect) should be pushed through the bird from vent to head.

Make sure the aerial is of a good length – approximately 6 to 7 feet.

50

A piece of wire (coat hanger wire is perfect) is pushed through crop area.

Some arable fields are now huge, like this 130-acre 'prairie', so that decoys may appear 'lost'.

Final adjustments!

individual pigeon shooter feels that he has a need for a flapper cradle or that he has always benefited from using one, then fine, I would not argue with that. In the end we acquire the equipment we feel we need and organise our sport the way we want, because that is our free choice.

Instead of a flapper I use a piece of aerial which is pushed up through the vent of a bird into the head. A piece of wire is pushed through the crop area of the bird and lodged in the first joint of each wing, which, incidentally, should not be broken. The decoy is then set into the wind at an angle of 45 degrees.

It takes only a slight breeze to set the bird rising and falling in a very realistic manner and it certainly beats pulling string! Strangely enough, this bird which is almost constantly moving and presented permanently with outstretched wings, appears to be constantly effective and seldom deters

pigeons from coming in, unlike the over-use of a flapper. The one time it may frighten our quarry is when there is absolutely no wind at all and the decoy bird remains perfectly motionless. On these occasions I refrain from presenting a bird in this way.

If a suitable piece of aerial or old fishing rod cannot be found then cane or a 'whippy' stick from the hedge may be employed, but these do not have the same qualities that an aerial has and the decoy does not move in such an effective manner.

I should say that a bird will revolve very easily, especially on a straight piece of aerial or cane thrust through it. The answer to this problem is to drill a block of wood and glue it to the business end of the aerial. It should then be shaped so that it is full-bodied enough to stop a bird rotating, streamlined enough to pass into the bird, and pointed enough to be thrust up into the

A decoy mounted on aerial is set in the decoy pattern. I prefer this method to using a flapper.

head. The photograph will illustrate more easily than words exactly what I mean.

I have had some very good shoots which were started with just three shell decoys made from real birds and incorporating the rocker spring I described earlier, plus one dead bird displayed on my length of aerial.

Real Birds

So far I have written about artificial decoys and various means of displaying these, and dead pigeons which have either been freshly shot or taken on a previous day. Of all the decoys one can use, dead birds are by far the most effective. It is true to say that I have seldom found birds reluctant to come into a pattern of them. Occasionally when birds seem wary, there are other factors which may be spooking them besides the decoys and I will write of these in another section.

Certainly, when the birds are really flighting, I have seldom, if ever, in all the years I have been pigeon shooting, found that they would not come to real bird decoys on drilling. It is true to say that un-cooperative rape pigeon will not play ball and refuse to be tempted by anything, though with pigeon on rape the fact which determines success or failure is not the decoy being used but the fact that the birds have totally changed their line of flight, have chosen a different spot altogether or are just not on the feed.

Having said that real birds are the most effective decoy you can employ, the question for most amateur pigeon shooters is, how to save enough birds from a previous shoot, which may have been a week or two earlier, for the day on which you require them. The answer is of course that you can't, unless you take birds from the freezer each time you shoot, use them as decoys and then throw them away, which seems a terribly wasteful way of carrying on.

One way of enhancing plastic shell decoys, for example, is to stick pigeon wings and tail feathers on to them. This is really quite effective and I had a selection of decoys thus adapted at one time which served me very well. If you do not wish to go to the trouble of using adhesive to stick the wings on, then they may be held in place quite simply with elastic bands. All this, however, is to go only half-way towards the ultimate aim, which is to make your own decoys using the material that nature has perfected as the most attractive to a pigeon – another pigeon.

Preserving dead birds as decoys is an art that has been practised for many years, indeed WAGBI (now BASC) had an advisory leaflet on how to do just that. Most methods advocated for making real bird decoys describe basically the mummification of the whole bird, involving the evisceration of the bird and the injection of formalin into its soft tissue – the eyes, brain and wing muscles, for example. All this called for very nearly the skills of a taxidermist. Preserving birds, or any creature come to that, takes care, time and patience. It is small wonder that few pigeon shooters have ever latched on to making their own decoys from the material at hand.

I am interested in fly fishing, and although I have a good command of the technical skills of casting I am the country's least successful fisherman. Despite this I well know the appeal of trout fishing and, having a father who is very adept at this sport and its accompanying skills, I also know that dedicated trout fishermen gain great satisfaction from tying their own flies.

It is worth asking if pigeon shooters, whose own sport is so much like trout fishing, are less patient or less interested in their sport than fishermen. Of course they are not, and dedicated pigeon shooters are just as interested in decoys as the fly fisherman is in the various fly patterns. This being the case, although there will always be those who are content with whatever is commercially available, there will also be those who will take pleasure from making equipment and trying its effectiveness in the field.

For anyone with a modicum of patience, a little skill and a bit of time, I am pleased to pass on a method of making shell decoys from real birds. These shells, if treated with care, will last for years and are as effective as using real birds. I am grateful to Maurice Richardson once again for being generous enough to share with a wider public techniques which he originally perfected for his own use.

Maurice toyed with the idea of using real birds for decoy making and for making them less of a hassle to prepare and preserve. The result has been a shell decoy which is relatively straightforward to make and which may perform *better* than a real bird because it can be caused to move naturally and continuously in a simple manner and by using the wind as a driving force.

Shell Decoys from Real Birds

Fly fishermen, as I said before, think nothing of making their own lures. I am sure that many pigeon shooters have the same aspiration but possibly do not know how to go about it. I have shown the results of Maurice Richardson's method to other shooters who have been impressed by it, for in the end there is no substitute for a decoy such as this.

The materials and tools you will require are:

Formaldehyde (purchased by the litre)
Rubber gloves
Very sharp knife
Scissors and 'tin snips'
Clean rag or tissue
Sawdust
½ inch paint brush and small artist's brush

Setting up a real bird shell decoy with a Richardson Rocker.

With the rocker in place, the bird assumes a natural position.

A handful of real bird shell decoys being set out on oil seed rape.

Wooden blocks for flexible peg (i.e. Richardson Rocker)
Wood adhesive
Supports for inside of carcass and for holding head in position.

Use only clean birds with unbroken wings. Use plenty of sawdust on the work surface so that feathers do not get soiled with blood.

1. Lay the bird on its back and remove the feathers from the breast.
2. Use a sharp knife and cut the skin along the breast bone.
3. Push the skin down as far as possible, leaving the breast meat exposed.
Using your sharp knife, cut away all the exposed flesh. This can be saved for culinary purposes and frozen if not immediately required.
4. Cut away the breast bone, ribs and legs using the 'tin snips' and remove all the bird's entrails.
5. Clean the inside of the carcass with rag or tissue and remove any traces of flesh which may be left. At this stage the carcass will be very floppy.
6. Put on rubber gloves and paint the inside of the bird with formaldehyde, using the ½ inch brush, making sure that all parts are covered. Then with the small artist's brush open the bird's beak and paint formaldehyde well inside the bird's throat, in fact right the way through.
Please note: Do not use too much formaldehyde – an eggcupful should do about four or five birds. Try not to spill any on the bird's feathers as this will mark.
7. When the bird has been thoroughly treated, place it over a support. Inventive minds come up with their own solution, but a section of plastic piping is ideal. The bird should be set to the required shape. A piece of wire through the neck may be advantageous at this stage. The head should be supported – a large nut is as handy as anything.

8. The decoy should be flattened out to look as large and as wide as possible as they do shrink and can become quite narrow if you do not do this. Having prepared the decoy, put it away in a secure, dry place, away from the prying eyes and hands of children.

Always use rubber gloves when working with formaldehyde, and make sure that you use it in a well ventilated place. Wash off with water immediately if any gets into contact with your own skin. To minimise the risk of accident, only pour out a small amount at a time. Birds which have been prepared by the described method will take about three to four weeks to cure. They may be left longer if you are not sure. When cured they will be rigid and are ready for the final preparation.
A wooden block of the type illustrated in the photograph should be stuck in position along the breast bone line within the empty body cavity of the bird. This block is for the insertion of the rocker peg, which is, by the way, a removable item and is only set in place when required for use.
As a matter of cosmetic look rather than function, although I personally think it adds strength, Maurice recommends painting the inside of the decoy with wood glue and sprinkling it with sawdust. The wooden block should be given time to set firmly.
These decoys will last several years with care, and even after becoming 'tatty' and even losing their heads, will still prove to be effective. If it rains it pays to bring them in and keep them dry. Shooters to whom I have described this method of making decoys have told me that they have sprayed their decoys with hairspray which acts slightly as a waterproofing agent and also keeps the feathers in place. It is an amusing thought, is it not, that the last notion an incoming pigeon might ever have on its mind is which decoy is wearing Harmony Hairspray!
Maurice carries his shell decoys in a

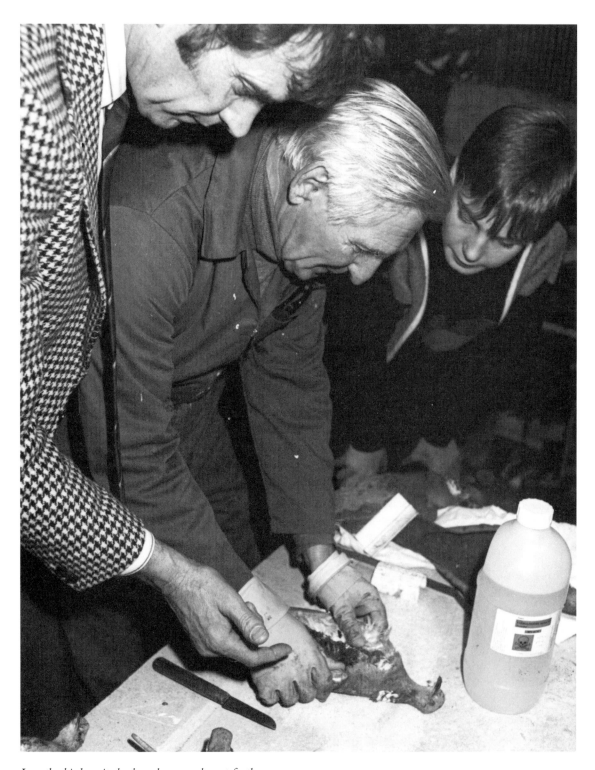

Lay the bird on its back and remove breast feathers.

Cut away breast flesh and remove breast bones, ribs and innards.

Scrape away as much flesh as possible.

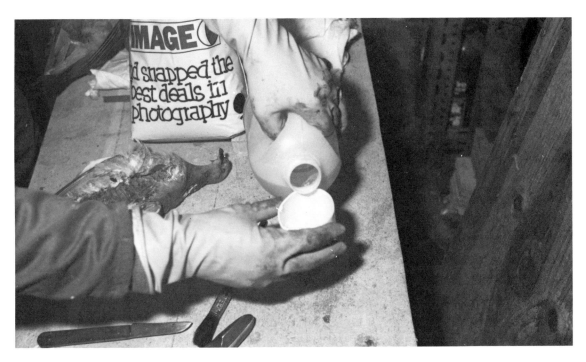

Do not pour too much formaldehyde at one time. Wear rubber gloves for safety.

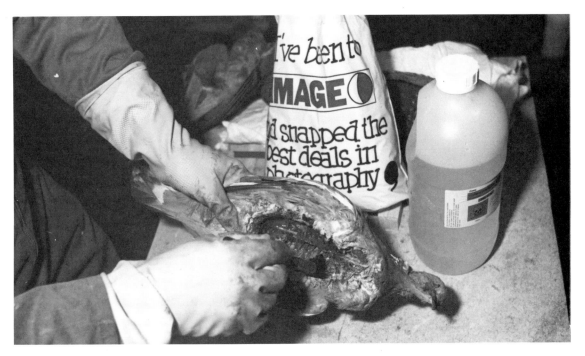

Use a paint brush to treat the bird with formaldehyde.

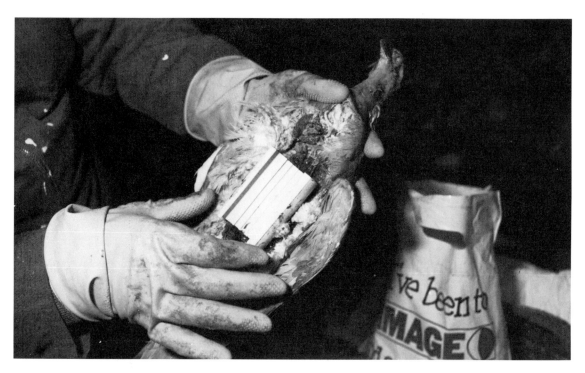

Use supports for the body shape.

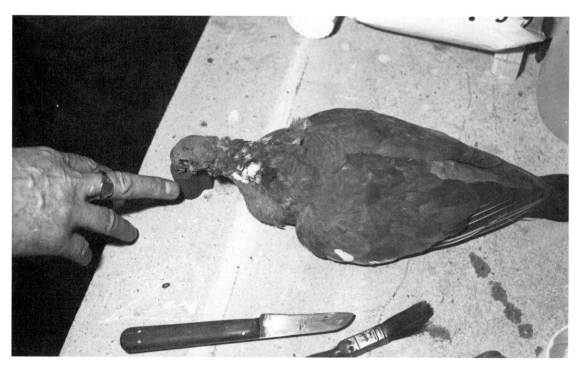

It is important to support the head at the correct, natural height.

62

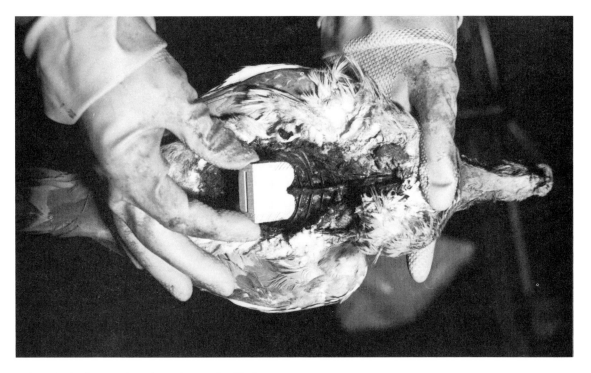

When the bird is cured, stick in the wooden block.

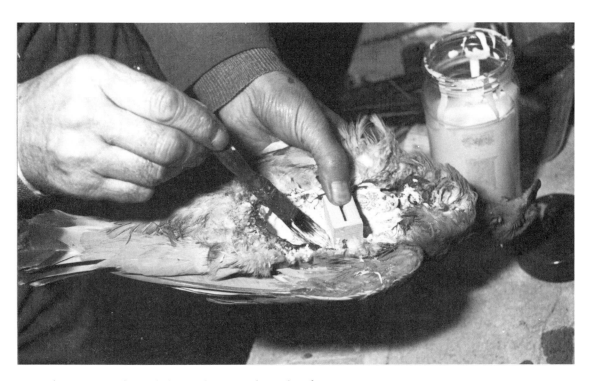

Paint the interior with wood glue, and cover with sawdust for cosmetic purposes – this also adds strength.

plastic container which also serves as a seat. Whichever way you decide to carry these decoys, they should certainly not be stuffed just any old how into a sack or bag with other equipment, as they just will not stand that sort of treatment. Brute force and ignorance is definitely out. A fly fisherman treats his equipment with a certain care and reverence. I am sure that we pigeon shooters are just as careful, especially when time has been invested in producing something of such value to ourselves as these decoys will inevitably prove to be.

4 Setting Up

Hides

When you really think about it pigeon shooting is a strange sort of hunting sport, for although the hunter seeks out the places being frequented by his quarry, the birds are then induced to come to the hunter so that he might bring them to book from a fixed position. Pigeon decoying is really all one big confidence trick. The artificial flock is used to induce pigeons to come into shotgun range and the hunter is disguised behind a hide which may be constructed of camouflage netting designed to simulate naturally growing foliage.

When I first started pigeon shooting I always made a natural hide. Being a country boy I had learned the skill of building a hide as a youngster when my friends and I would spend hours building secret dens. Without doubt the best pigeon shooting hide is the one constructed from the natural materials found on the spot.

During the late spring to early autumn, making a hide with whatever material is naturally occurring is usually fairly straightforward. When there are leaves on the trees and bushes a hide can quickly be made from one or two well foliaged branches. In the winter it is less easy of course.

Before I carried camouflage netting I used to stick a few branches in the ground, with a hedge as background, and tear up tufts of dead grass from the ditch edge or hedgerow margin. I would then fluff out this grass over my supporting sticks. It is surprising how far even a fairly small amount will go.

Farms have become in general very tidy places and I found over the years an increasing difficulty in obtaining hide making material. Well trimmed hedges, tidy ditches and an increasing shortage of rough corners limited the opportunity to build good natural hides in many places. This shortage of natural materials and the need to be mobile has made the use of camouflage netting invaluable.

With suitable supports, purpose-made light hide poles being the obvious choice, a few pieces of camouflage netting will make an adequate hide very quickly. It is advisable when there are natural materials to hand to include these in breaking up the somewhat stark outlines of the netting. When natural cover presents itself for either hide making or just straightforward concealment, I would always recommend the use of this before employing nets. In general my hides tend to be made of a basis of netting with some adornment of grass or other foliage.

I was shooting over stubble during the late summer and had made a net hide against a hedge. I was using a mixture of real bird shell decoys and dead birds. My hide was situated right under the main pigeon flight and there was a steady stream of birds. Something, however, seemed to be spooking the birds and they just would not come within range. I was surprised since the decoys seemed perfect and I was well concealed.

I became suspicious that the hide was to blame as it appeared just a little too dark and conspicuous against the hedgerow, the colours of which were beginning to mellow with the lateness of the summer. Slightly off-line and about seventy yards further along the field the hedge became considerably higher and wider. I decided to conceal myself right inside this hedge without using

Building a hide using netting and grass.

any artificial material whatsoever. I made my move and set up shop as described. It was very interesting to watch the birds veer off course and come confidently into the decoys. I eventually made a modest bag. Quite obviously on that day under the conditions which prevailed my hide netting was acting as a deterrent and inhibiting the pigeons from coming in with confidence.

When using nets it is important to bear in mind that they will not always look right to pigeon eyes so try to enhance the appearance with any available natural foliage. Nets will also billow in a wind and steps should be taken to ensure this does not happen by tying or pegging.

I am pleased to see that Sporting Developments of Fife have now made available a new netting which is called Grass Screen and is olive brown on one side

and a pale green on the other – most lightweight netting is dark green. Grass Screen should prove invaluable not only to pigeon shooters but to wildfowlers as well, who require subdued muted coloration for use on the marsh.

It is incredible to think that some shooters are still carrying bulky old-fashioned netting adorned with hessian scrim. Enough to make a decent hide will fill a sack and is quite heavy. The name of the game is to keep weight to a minimum. This is why I recommend the modern netting, although as I have mentioned elsewhere, it is certainly not cheap.

Maurice Richardson has a piece of hessian with an upper band of netting. This makes a light, effective and not too bulky hide, so for anyone anxious to keep cost to a minimum this may well be a useful idea.

A hessian hide with an upper band of netting.

Whatever type of hide you choose it is useful to incorporate some sort of overhead cover without inhibiting your shooting. Birds passing or approaching at a height can look right into a hide with inadequate background or with a lack of some overhead covering. A draped piece of netting will solve this problem.

A hide should have an adequate 'shooting window'. It should also be large enough for smooth gun mounting since there is nothing worse than bringing the gun up to engage an incoming pigeon only to snag the netting and consequently miss the chance of a shot.

Hide Discipline

It is advisable to sit in a hide since quite long waits can be experienced. Shooting from a sitting position is the preferred method, but some shooters find it better to rise to shoot. The height of the hide must be considered in relation to the method an individual chooses to shoot. If you shoot from a sitting position and the hide is slightly too high, you will most probably mount the gun with the head high, and experience a higher proportion of misses.

Not every shooter has the discipline to wait patiently in a hide. I have seen them all in my time, ranging from the 'I want to get out to stretch my legs' type to the constantly standing up, fidgeting and peering over the top sorts. It *does* take patience to wait for pigeon, especially when action is slow. Anyone who cannot bear periods of relative inactivity should take up a different type of shooting. I never consider time spent in a hide is wasted, even when a shoot has not proved very profitable. I have included a section of memorable moments within this book to prove the point.

My wife has often said that she cannot understand the appeal of 'sitting around in ditches like a vagrant'. I have spent years telling her how much more to it there is than that, and I think I am now finally managing to convince her of the truth of this. She was very amused to hear from another pigeon shooter at the Game Fair that his wife thought that sitting around in cold damp fields was 'absolutely ridiculous'. Perhaps this is most ladies' perception of our sport, and at the risk of being labelled as sexist, I must venture that the sport does seem to have an appeal exclusively for the male of the species. I have only ever met one lady pigeon shooter in my life.

In whatever way you choose to conceal yourself, the important question is where to site the hide. The answer is that the birds should tell you. The birds will often favour a particular part of a field, and this may be determined by the land's sheltered qualities or the condition of the crop.

Observation

I will usually go to where the birds are working and try to get under their main approach line. This means that you should not be in too much of a hurry to get on to a field and set up. Just watching and observing will determine the best place to situate the hide and will obviate the necessity to move if you do not get it right the first time.

If a mistake is made in the initial setting up there is always a good deal of bother involved in moving, so reading the signs and getting it right the first time is quite important. At times, however, the birds will spontaneously change their line. This should prompt you to move, as it really is a mistake not to bother. We are all lazy at times but to sit it out rather than to put the effort into moving to a more hopeful location can mean the difference between

making a decent bag and possibly nothing at all.

When a field is immense and the birds have been pushed to a secluded corner, if you are shooting in company, one of the partnership will probably find it profitable to take himself off to find a spot which will enable him to keep the birds on the move to the advantage of both himself and his partner. I have described incidents of this ploy elsewhere in the book and would merely reiterate here that it can be well worth pursuing.

You will notice that I do not appear to advocate bale hides. This is because to the modern pigeon shooter they are largely irrelevant. Most farmers who will spare bales for hides put them only on oil seed rape. They then render these hides useless by placing banger guns close by them, hence birds become jumpy and suspicious of this type of hide. Bale hides are seldom placed where you can make best use of them anyway. I have stated several times the need for a pigeon shooter to be mobile and so this is why I prefer hides which can be quickly and easily erected.

A hide does not always have to be all that substantial. If drab clothing is worn and the hands and face are covered, then a minimum of cover may be employed as long as you remain motionless.

Safety

When you site a hide, safety factors should be uppermost in your mind – safety that is for yourself and for the general public. Hides in thorn bushes, particularly blackthorn, can be hazardous for the shooter. Blackthorn will spike into you deeply and may prove to be extremely difficult to get out. They do tend to poison human flesh quite readily. I have a slightly misshapen left thumb which is the result of the deep entry of a thorn about four years ago, which I never did get out. It must have eventually dissolved away in me.

A bird is shot from a bale hide. Note proximity to hedgerow and tree.

Some years ago I was just climbing into a hide made of natural materials in a hawthorn hedge when a 'whippy' twig caught me across the eye. It was extremely painful and my vision was badly obscured. There were patches of snow lying around and so I rubbed snow into my eye to numb the severe irritation.

I was foolishly determined not to be driven home so I stuck it out and shot 28 pigeons with one eye clenched tightly shut. The intense cold began to affect my un-injured eye, which was under a certain amount of strain since it was functioning alone, so, as I had to drive home, I decided discretion was the better part of valour and packed up.

When I got home I received a great deal of deserved chiding from my wife and a visit to the doctor's was arranged. My own doctor sent me to the city hospital eye department where they were at first fearful that a thorn had entered my eyeball. Fortunately it had not, but I had in fact scratched the cornea. The result was a period of time spent with that eye bandaged so as not to put undue strain upon it. Apparently damage of this nature can cause a traumatic cataract. I reiterate, thorn hedges can be dangerous so be mindful of your eyes.

Personal safety is one thing but the safety of others should be paramount in your mind. Siting hides close to well-used footpaths or bridlepaths is not to be recommended. Similarly if you are shooting perhaps across a field corner, towards a hedgerow, it means that there is no way of knowing who may be approaching out of sight. The old adage, 'Never shoot where you can't see' must always apply.

I would never shoot towards a road, even one two hundred yards away, as shot will carry much further than many people think.

69

Although it may have lost its ability to harm, shot pattering down following a loud report is no way to endear the shooter to the general public and we should all bear in mind the public relations angle of our sport.

There are times when a shooter finds it necessary to leave the hide and whatever the reason, be it to carry out a natural bodily function or to set up dead birds as decoy, it is highly desirable to remove the cartridges from the gun. Anything, it might be the wind or the dog, could cause a loaded gun to fall over and discharge itself, with disastrous consequences. Many years ago a cousin of my father's placed his shotgun against a fence while he opened a gate to let sheep through. The sheep knocked the gun over and it fell at a particular angle against the gate, discharged, and killed the young man.

Accidents can occur out of the blue; they are very often the result of human error, carelessness or lack of judgement. A shotgun wound incurred at short distance is invariably fatal, so play safe; it is just not worth the risk to be blasé when in possession of a weapon.

There have been many occasions when I have had the chance of a shot, perhaps even a double, and there has merely been a click because after removing the cartridges before doing something outside the hide, I have forgotten to put them back on returning. But this is surely a small annoyance when weighed against safety.

It is also important to be careful not to get soil or snow up the barrels of the gun because to fire it with such an obstruction can cause a burst, with disastrous results. Being ultra-careful in this respect is no bad fault and it pays to get into the habit of regularly looking through the barrels of your gun when shooting from a hide.

Hide Siting

Finding the right spot is the key to making a good shoot from a hide. Good reconnaissance and observation will decide where you should set up for operations, then the next step is obviously to set out a pattern of decoys. I have dealt with lofting decoys in an earlier section but it is worth stressing again here the importance of those trees which are well favoured by pigeons. These trees will pull birds which, after alighting, drop down to feed in the general area a few yards away. A hide at the other end of the field with as effective a pattern of decoys as you like will not affect the birds' natural inclination to follow the sequence they have built up for feeding on that field.

It is worth stressing that a hide right at the base of a tree, although affording good background, may often be counter-productive for the shooter. Birds coming into a tree can present an incredibly difficult target for anyone hidden beneath its canopy, even when there is no leaf. As I have said on previous occasions though, trees are welcome especially under today's conditions as they allow you the opportunity to get those decoys up where they will be seen. Years ago I never bothered, today under many conditions it is essential.

There have been occasions when I have set out with six dead birds as decoys and have not set one on the ground but lofted every one in those attractive trees. I had a useful little shoot under way on a sowing of spring beans which started off in this manner. The first twenty birds came to the decoys I had lofted. The angle for shooting was quite difficult and eventually I had enough birds to persuade the incoming pigeons that the flock on the floor were really on to quite a good thing. The shoot progressed in a conventional way and I ended up with nearly fifty.

I have described elsewhere how you may also place decoys on fence posts besides lofting in trees. However, most decoys are required down on the field. Setting up decoys is not a great exercise and carries no mystique.

A hide directly under a tree is often best avoided.

Setting Out Decoys

A young acquaintance who once came shooting with me on a memorable Good Friday when we had a bag well in excess of a hundred birds, but for goodness knows how many cartridges, once said that he had seen the patterns I advocated for setting out decoys in a magazine article and that he had been forced to smile. I asked him why and he replied that it was all very well having patterns in mind for setting out the decoys but that he had been shooting pigeons successfully all his life and he never paid any mind to any pattern. In essence, what he said he did was to take eight or ten frozen pigeon from the freezer when he had a shoot in mind, and when he was in position on the field he just scattered them about like the old-fashioned way of sowing corn. Where the birds fell they stayed, whether they were faced down or face up it made no difference as it seemed to work just the same.

I cannot disagree with his assessment in general. Firstly the most important factor is to find the place where the pigeons want to be. Having found this spot, very often the initial decoy pattern is immaterial, since the birds are returning to a place where they really want to feed. Pigeons on their backs will not always make incoming birds turn away, so my young friend's method is not so haphazard as may at first appear.

When I set out decoys I also distribute them in the 'sowing corn' method but I do

71

have a sort of pattern in mind. I fancy that even my acquaintance, experienced pigeon shooter that he is, has a pattern subconsciously in his mind as he throws out his decoys.

Wind

The direction of the wind dictates the approach of the pigeons to the decoy pattern. Birds will inevitably come in to land *against* the wind even if they have made their initial approach *on* the wind.

Some experts advocate a horseshoe pattern of decoys with a 'killing area' encircled by the edges of the horseshoe. Basically I would agree with this, although I would rather describe myself as an amateur pigeon shooting specialist. When the wind is blowing across my position or is at an angle from left or right, then certainly a horseshoe, or a variation thereof, is as good a pattern as any to have in mind. When the wind is directly in my back I like to have the decoys in two 'blocks' with an empty approach channel through the middle. The word block, however, denotes symmetry, which is something the pattern should not have. I always try to make sure as I add to my pattern that it does not become too symmetrical in shape. It is all too easy for the human brain to organise decoys in a way that a creature such as the pigeon does not perceive as natural.

Knowing the wind direction and the way decoys have accordingly been set, means that you will know the general presentation of most of the incoming targets. Birds will come to the decoys frequently on the same line. I know from experience that when I pick up after a good shoot, most birds lie in two or three concentrations with a minority scattered here and there, which to my mind proves the point.

More important than the general pattern, I feel, is how close to present the decoys and the direction in which they face. Birds do not feed with their backs into the wind

because this ruffles the feathers and the bird loses body heat. In general birds feed into the wind, but if you look at a living flock feeding, the birds are pecking here and there, so some are facing across the wind.

When putting out decoys it is important to try to make your artificial flock look as natural as possible. Avoiding symmetry, and placing the birds in different directions are therefore essential. It is also important not to place your decoys too close together – ten or twelve feet is close enough. If I am setting off with a handful of decoys or so, then I would certainly place my decoys further apart than even this distance.

As birds are shot reinforcing the pattern with these fresh birds is accepted as good practice. A stick wedged under the chin is still as good a method as any of setting up dead birds, although wire frames of the type previously described are useful. I always try to set my birds in a head-down feeding position, which denotes all is well.

Some pigeon shooters feel that if they shoot a bird which then falls on its back amongst the decoys, it will act as a deterrent, so they insist on putting every one the right way up. Certainly fallen birds which are the 'wrong' way up may at times deter, but frequently it makes no difference whatsoever.

The question of feathers lying around I would answer in a similar way. Pigeons are loose-plumaged birds and feathers fly freely at times. I often pick up any really concentrated patches of feathers, especially on drilling, but again, to be honest, I think that generally they make very little difference. We humans try to shorten the odds by having everything as right as we can make it hence our obsession at times with feathers and birds upside-down.

The number of decoys you should actually set up is debatable. The most I have ever set up 'properly' was seventy. If birds have fallen face down in a roughly suitable place, to be honest, I leave them where they are. I may set up the first twenty or thirty birds I

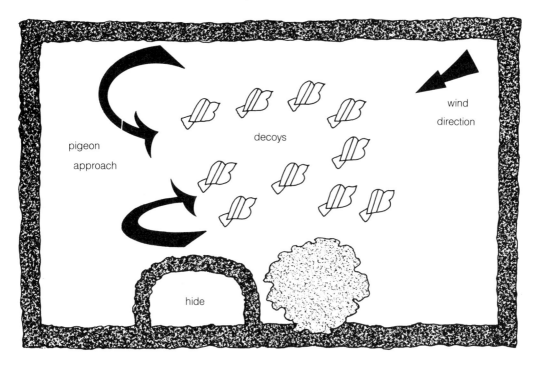

(a)

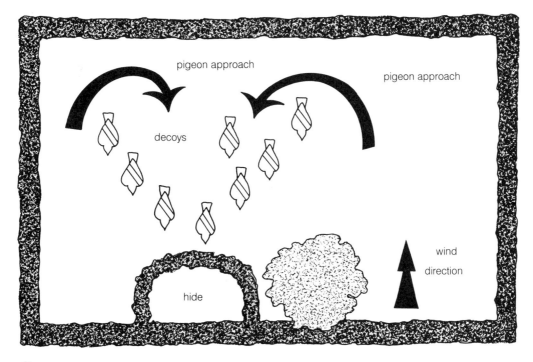

(b)

Decoy patterns in relation to the wind.

Do not set decoys too close together.

have shot and thereafter possibly only move birds either to expand the breadth of my pattern, to turn them the right way up or to spread the density somewhat and to clear my killing area, which might be becoming cluttered.

There is another occasion when I move birds, and that is if the wind direction changes. So often the wind is variable and when this occurs then adjusting the decoys is important. I dislike having the wind directly into my face when I am in a hide. The reason for this is that birds will tend to come to the decoys directly from behind and over the top of you, which means that they are a fair way out before they are spotted. I like to present my birds at an optimum killing range so this does not fall in with that philosophy.

There are times when you cannot avoid having the wind in your face. When this happens I recommend that the decoys are set much further out than normal and to the side, not directly in front of you. This way you can shoot birds swinging round to come into the decoys, or catch them crossing to the side.

I have often read recommendations that decoys should be set out 15 – 40 yards from the hide. I do not agree with this totally and neither does my friend Maurice Richardson – if the wind is in your face, yes, but when the wind is not then we do not think that this is altogether advisable.

Maurice believes that many of his decoys are as close as 8 yards and that as a general rule his decoy pattern is not very far out at all. In general I would agree with this. A decoy pattern with its furthest away birds at 40 yards distance may attract birds in with the intention of settling at the far side of the pattern, hence they will be in excess of 40 yards range for shooting. It is my contention that birds in excess of 40 yards, although killable and technically still within range of a twelve bore and standard load cartridges, are not in what I would call an *optimum* range. Optimum range is that distance at which most birds can be *consistently* killed by the average shot.

Distance

The average distance a decoyed pigeon is killed at is no more than 20 yards and I have spent some time calculating this to prove the point. I would state with some conviction that the birds in a decoy pattern should be set with the nearest as close as 7 or 8 yards from the hide and the furthest at no more than 25–30 yards and there is no advantage in setting birds further out than this in most decoying circumstances. Incidentally I always place my mounted decoys with outstretched wings at the point of the pattern. This is as good a spot as any for the flapper if you choose to employ one.

The whole point with decoy patterns is that you are trying to simulate a living, feeding, flock. To my mind quality of decoy is as important as quantity. A few lofted birds, a couple set on fence posts, a few real bird shells nodding away with everything else you shoot as reinforcements, is beginning to get as close to reality, I feel, as it is possible to achieve.

In this sport of pigeon shooting two factors which must weigh heavily for success to be consistently attained are: to use your eyes and to learn from experience. An old Chinese proverb states, 'That which we buy with experience never devalues'. Those old Chinese were certainly very wise, for there is truly no substitute for experience in the end.

An experienced pigeon shooter can make a shoot from nothing if the opportunity arises and I know people who take pleasure in doing just that. I have done this myself on occasions and it can be very satisfying.

One October I was rough shooting on a friend's farm and had bagged a hare and a brace of pheasant. As I worked along a hedge with the dog, I noticed pigeons in a line of trees in the opposite hedge. I found that the birds were still motionless in the trees as I came closer, so I dropped down into the ditch and made a stealthy approach. I managed to get within 50 yards before the birds broke like a cloudburst in all directions. I ducked low out of sight and sure enough some of those scattering pigeons came straight over me. I dropped two and my shots caused a flurry of birds from the stubble on the far side of the field. Hugging the ditch bottom I had a short interlude of fast and furious shooting in which I collected a total of six birds. I proceeded up the hedge and over on to the stubble. It should have been ploughed under long ago, but still remained because of pressure of work on my friend who runs his 250 acres single-handed. Birds were still on the wing so I set out my six fresh birds as decoys and found a super ready-made hide within a fallen branch through which grass had grown tall. I had a lively pigeon shoot that afternoon and called a halt only when I saw parties of duck dipping on the stubble by a little pond across the other side of the field. I took myself off and ended the day with six duck in the bag as well. As I've said before, you have to be an opportunist in pigeon shooting and certainly this applies to rough shooting as well.

Shooting Sitting

Shooting from a hide is unlike most other types of shooting inasmuch as many shots are taken from a sitting position, indeed, from some particularly cramped hides I have hastily erected, I have shot kneeling.

Hide discipline is important and looking *through* the net is vital. Pigeons being as sharp-sighted as they are, will invariably spot a nice, shiny, luminous human face peering over the top of the hide a mile off.

Most inexperienced pigeon shooters do not let approaching birds come close enough in, at least not for a second shot. I let

Set the decoy with outstretched wings at the head of the pattern.

birds come well in so that I have a better than evens chance of one and a good opportunity for a second. If birds are committed to land, I see no reason not to shoot one on the ground and a second as it departs – after all I've done the hard part which is to get them there.

I once had a bird land right out beyond my decoys and decided not to shoot as it appeared to be at extreme range. Moments later a second bird landed, closer this time but still a fair way out. I judged, however, that this bird was in range. I lined up on it and fired. Imagine my surprise when both birds flipped over, stone dead. I stepped out the distances and found the nearest bird to be 45 paces and the furthest bird to be at 63. Since I am over 6 feet tall we can assume that those paces equated with yards. Not bad for $1\frac{1}{16}$ oz of seven shot I might add! Incidentally, Maurice has been using nine shot and found them deadly on decoyed pigeon. I have also used them and detected no significant difference on pigeon over decoys – interesting when you think there are still those who believe that the only cartridge for pigeon is $1\frac{1}{8}$ oz of six shot or even fives!

Shooting from a Hide

Many average shots can kill *a* pigeon when the opportunity offers itself; shooting *two* appears to create difficulties. Knocking down a few doubles certainly helps to swell the bag but apart from that, and the satisfaction of being able to do it, there is no particular merit in it. After all many people have successfully pursued pigeon with a single barrelled shotgun, myself included.

When several pigeons or, as sometimes happens, a large party of pigeon appear over the decoys, the shooter often becomes indecisive. He chooses a bird, changes his mind, mis-mounts his gun, checks, and then misses with both barrels! Shooting should always be smooth, unhurried and instinctive; it is, therefore, not easy to break down the sequence of events leading to a successful 'double'. I will refrain from saying right and left since many shooters use over-under shotguns, and try to go through the sequence as I see it.

First, choose a bird, concentrate on it and shoot it, but as you are doing this you may have picked a likely second bird; if you have do *not* dwell on it. Changing your mind about the first bird at this stage is probably going to cause a double miss. If the first bird is on its way down, after you have fired swing on to your second bird which may well be jinking and taking speedy evasive action. Make sure your barrels are well through before firing.

I have often picked my first bird, fired, swung confidently on to my second, and dropped it efficiently – only to find that my first bird is still flying. Still, no matter, it proves I suppose that I am shooting instinctively. I believe that once we start thinking too much about what we are doing, a higher percentage of misses occurs. Incidentally, I am an advocate of keeping both eyes open and looking at the bird. Consciously sighting with the barrels should not enter into it at all if the gun is being mounted well.

Disposal of the Bag

Most reasonably competent pigeon shooters bag more birds than can be used for their own culinary purposes. Handling shot birds in a careful way, so that they remain saleable, is a real consideration as the birds represent a small return to set against expenditure on cartridges, which can be quite high. First of all let me say that I do not welcome high prices for pigeon. A high price encourages the shooting of pigeon for purely mercenary reasons and this is neither good for the birds or the true value of our sport. A reasonable return is welcome, however, and we should be grateful that pigeon are saleable, for if they were not then the sport would have to be viewed in a different way.

To put this in another way, I am a hunter first and foremost and, although I do not eat all I shoot, it is sufficient for me to know that someone will make good use of my surplus. If pigeons were not saleable then I would approach my shooting of them in a different manner. I would shoot pigeon when they presented themselves as part of a rough shoot but certainly the attraction of decoying and shooting large numbers would diminish somewhat. Remember, I am speaking entirely personally. To shoot large quantities of a creature which I could not dispose of for a useful purpose, would reduce the sport to that of killing for killing's sake, and I would be hard put to justify it.

To say that control of pigeon numbers was sufficient justification for killing them would not be enough for me, I am afraid, because I view myself in the first place as a sportsman and not a pest controller. This is purely a personal view and other folk may have a different philosophy towards the sport. It could be argued that ratting is a field sport and yet no one ever eats the bag derived from that sport. I would argue that the rat is a major public menace and killing it needs not further justification beyond the fact that it is vermin, but, as I said in my introduction, I do not view woodpigeons in that way. I am sure that foxhunters would understand such reasoning. Foxes are pests, there are many of them and they are inedible, but they are also a valuable sporting asset on the country scene. However, I am sure the pleasure of hunting them would diminish if it was possible to catch dozens in a day, for then the foxhunter would become a pest controller and not a sportsman.

True wildfowlers take pleasure in bagging a few geese for their own, or friends', requirements. The sale of wild geese is forbidden by law in Britain so when so-called 'cowboys' indulge in a gratuitous slaughter of geese, more principled sportsmen are incensed by a wanton act which cannot even be slightly justified by being carried out for mercenary purposes. If we are unsure of the purity of our own motives when we pursue wild creatures, then we will find it increasingly difficult to justify their pursuit for sport to a citizenry which can at times be swayed by a sentimentalism towards wildlife, which our opponents actively fuel.

Most woodpigeons sold by sportsmen in Britain end up exported to the Continent, since the British market is relatively small. The overseas market is affected by a seasonal demand and so we see fluctuations in the price paid by game dealers for pigeon. When birds are being bought for placing in cold storage, the price is obviously low. When sales are moving again, the price rises and quite often there is a premium paid for fresh birds. I have often received more than double the price from my dealer for the fresh birds I have taken to him over the frozen birds which I have stored in my freezer. When fresh birds are making a premium it may be tempting to pass off thawed birds as fresh. A word of caution – game dealers can tell if this has occurred!

A freezer is a necessity for the regular pigeon shooter unless he has a channel for the quick disposal of his birds close at hand. The way we treat our bag is important so that the birds remain saleable. Birds shot in winter pose less of a problem than those shot in summer, since the process of putrefaction is naturally much slower under the cooler conditions. There is also an absence of blowflies.

In summer, flies will often lay their glistening white eggs around the beak and under the wings of shot pigeon. Birds thus affected can still be sold since heads may be removed without affecting the birds' saleable quality. Eggs in other places can be scraped off with the edge of a knife.

My game dealer tells me that it is useful to spread your bag of birds on a brick or concrete floor to cool down prior to freezing them. A garage floor is suitable in the absence of other outbuildings. Birds should be frozen in the feathers. I fold the wings neatly and tuck the head under, as this way more birds can be packed into the freezer and they do not freeze into untidy, space-consuming, grotesque shapes. When I sell these pigeons from the freezer they will travel for the 35-minute drive to my dealer perfectly well and on arrival go straight into his big freezers.

Birds which you intend to sell fresh should be taken to the dealer quickly. Warm birds in a heap or sacked up in plastic bags will deteriorate quite rapidly, especially in hot weather. Once they have become over-ripe and show discoloration round the vent area, your dealer will no longer want them; so the rule is, cool them down as quickly as possible and take them for sale as soon as you can.

Any pigeon which you intend to keep for your own purposes can be de-breasted and the two slabs of meat from either side of the breast bone may then be frozen until required for use. Pigeon meat is useful for a number of wholesome dishes ranging from pâté and casseroles to the inevitable pigeon pie. There are many good recipes available and some good game cookery books which will guide the culinary minded better than I, being merely a shooter of pigeon and not a cordon bleu chef. I have a friend, however, who has devised a few recipes for making pigeon into something rather special, and they are listed later.

5 Oil Seed Rape – The Big Challenge

Cropping Policies

The biggest change in cropping which has taken place on arable farms in this country from the 1950s onwards has undoubtedly been the large scale growing of oil seed rape. There is currently a move to reduce the acreage of this crop and to replace it with alternatives, but nonetheless a substantial acreage will continue to be grown. From the pigeon shooter's point of view shooting over this crop can be extremely frustrating and quite frequently unproductive, for although rape attracts large congregations of pigeon during the winter and early spring, they can be notoriously difficult to decoy.

Rape is sown in August and steadily establishes reasonable growth until late in the year. Pigeons do not really bother with it until December. It provides the opportunity to shoot pigeons at three stages of its existence. The first period extends from December to about April (occasionally May), when growth becomes rapid. The second period when shooting may be productive is in July or August, after the farmer has swathe-rowed the rape, that is, cut it into rows to ripen, prior to combining. Finally, the rape stubbles may prove an attraction for pigeon and are well worth observing.

I believe that oil seed rape has played a very important role in the development of pigeon shooting as a leading field sport. Pigeon shooting has always had a popular appeal I know, but the advent of rape made shooting more accessible for more people.

Farmers who are approached for shooting when their rape is attracting the attention of large numbers of birds, rarely, in my experience, say no. Anyone seeking pigeon shooting should bear this fact in mind. Permission will be more readily given when the rape is at its most vulnerable stage, which is during the winter when growth is minimal and during the early spring when it begins to grow again. Once access to a farm has been gained and the basic rules of good behaviour are adhered to, then it is feasible to expect that permission will be forthcoming for a continuation of shooting over the whole year on that farm. I owe most of my shooting to this crop, which has given me access to farms where I now have a chance to go rough shooting, duck shooting, or rabbiting.

It takes a dedicated shooter to turn out on the oil seed rape on many of the days experienced in Britain during the winter. Enthusiasm can wane, even in the keenest, when a day of sucking mud and knife-edged wind has resulted in less than a handful of birds. A decent sized bag of birds is well earned during the early months. I have had good bags in December, February, March, April and even May. January has always been a fairly lean time since snow and other adverse weather conditions often intervene.

Suitable Conditions

The greatest contributory factor towards making a good bag over rape is undoubtedly wind. I am always most optimistic if it is blowing well. Heavy rain is literally a wash-out; fog is usually an end to any hopes for a day's shooting, as is snow, at least for decoying; bright and frosty days without a hint of a breeze are mostly a dead loss. On still, frosty days birds can be observed sitting plum-like and motionless on the trees, conserving energy and digesting the rape with which they have packed their crops early on. These birds when disturbed will move a field or two away and descend on other likely resting trees from whence they are unlikely to return. If the birds are still feeding then they usually have the choice of another rape field not too far away where they may continue grazing undisturbed.

A point to bear in mind is that during the early part of the rape season, pigeon flight out to feed from the roosting woods at first light. A pigeon shooter arriving at his likely field at around eleven o'clock in the morning is going to encounter birds which have largely satiated their appetites and are consequently less than co-operative. It can be a useful ploy to be on a well-worked field very early before the birds flight out and to be ready with decoys set up for their arrival. This can be productive for about an hour but no one should expect a day's shooting on this basis.

Wind is a highly desirable factor in this sport. Other considerations include time of day, as I have said, the state of the crop, and knowing the favoured areas of individual fields. The birds' lines of approach to the field from the roosting or resting areas are very important and should be identified. It is less easy to spot these on still days when no definite flight line may be observed and birds are probably approaching at a high altitude and over a broad front.

On windy days birds will tend to use the features of the land along which to make their approach. A hedge line, row of trees, a stream or valley may signal a positive motorway for pigeon movement, so it is important to be positioned along and under this line of flight so that the decoys will be more easily spotted in what may be a sea of rape. Besides, birds know where they are heading for on a field, and it helps the shooter to know why. Cold exposed banks, open to the prevailing wind, are going to be avoided by the birds. Favoured spots are likely to be in the dips and hollows where it is sheltered or where the field runs to a thick, warm hedge line. There may well be a favoured line of trees which the birds use as a first staging post or digesting station. These can always be easily identified, being liberally splashed with dropping, as will be the ground beneath.

It sometimes pays, if the flight line has been clearly identified, to have your decoys not on the rape but on the field next door if the flight leads over it. If the neighbouring field is ploughed and fallow or even grass it can be a good ploy to set up on this since the decoys will be more clearly visible. This is something I frequently do.

December Shoot

One December afternoon, about four days before Christmas, I arrived to view a rape field at about 12.30. The farmer had told me that it was being badly mauled and this was my first opportunity to look at it. It was more or less a scouting trip although I had my equipment with me. I was able to drive right up to the field and parked on the little bridge which crossed the brook forming the boundary. The rape field lay to my left and straight in front of me was a field of grass. The only division between this field and the rape was a broken-down hedge which ran down towards me.

It was a damp afternoon with one of those rapidly changing skies. A burst of watery sunshine would be followed by a brief, sleety, shower. A strong wind blew from my left, which was approximately north-west. As I sat watching I realised that there was a steady trickle of birds battling in

The author contemplating a 'sea' of rape.

odd ones and twos across the grass to the rape. Without any particular enthusiasm I decided to spend an hour here so, loaded up with a minimum of gear, I trudged some hundred and fifty yards to the hedge. I set up my hide at the base of an old tree stump so as to obtain some shelter from the wind which was directly in my back. I broke up the starkness of my hide with handfuls of dead grass and leaves from the hedge bottom because I was very aware of how darkly it stood out against the background. This accomplished, I set up six dead birds which had been shot the evening before at roost. It was by now about ten past one.

The first birds took me by surprise since they came low and were incredibly difficult to spot against the meadow. It is surprising how quickly your eyes become accustomed to picking up incoming birds from a distance, and I was ready for the next two arrivals. Within a short while I had decided

that a bag of twenty, possibly thirty birds was going to be likely and felt pleased that I had quite a decent little shoot in hand. Every bird I shot joined the pattern. I had about fifty cartridges with me, the rest being in the car. I had not taken more since it had not seemed worth it. At about a quarter to two it was necessary to go back to my vehicle for more shells, for such had been the almost continuous stream of birds to come my way that ammunition immediately to hand was low.

I found that even if birds were not necessarily coming to my decoys, they would pull sufficiently off-line so as to come within range. My shots caused birds which had already passed on to the rape behind me to come racing back on the wind. Then I found that many of them would spot the decoys and swerve in on a tight circle to the birds I had set up.

December afternoons are incredibly

short-lived, as was this one. It was approaching dusk when the birds stopped coming. I picked up all the birds which lay in the field before me. Then I hunted the rape and hedgerow, which yielded a further goodly number. My low expectation of the afternoon had not been justified since I picked up 139 pigeons. I counted my cartridge cases and found that I had performed pretty well since there were only 174 empties. I had known through the afternoon that my shooting had been economical because at one point I had shot 20 birds straight without a miss. This shoot represents without doubt the best cartridge to kill ratio I have ever achieved, if I discount small kills of, say, five or six birds for five or six shots.

This day finished, incidentally, with a mini-drama. I discovered that I had omitted to bring my game carrriers with me and a search of the car revealed only a fairly inadequate hessian sack. I filled this with birds, as well as stuffing as many of them as I could into the bag with my nets. I slung all my equipment around me and, thus loaded, tried desperately to get the bag of birds up on to my shoulders. Inevitably, after much struggling, and swearing, the bag split. I realised more than one journey was going to be necessary so I set off back to the car with my equipment and some of the birds.

I loaded the car and looked back through the growing gloom to where the rest of the day's bag were waiting to be retrieved. It suddenly seemed a heck of a way back. I walked on to the field and tested it, surely it was not that bad? It felt quite firm really, well worth the risk of taking the car over. The physical exertion, the awareness of an increasing weariness and desire for food and a hot bath, clouded my judgement. I reached the birds I had left perfectly well with the car and, with a feeling of great relief, loaded them on. On the way back I failed to avoid a marshy spot and within seconds was down to the axles.

In the pitch dark I headed across the fields for the mile and a half to the farmhouse.

The farmer's son, with some mirth and good humour, came with a powerful tractor to pull me out, which I hasten to add was not easy and afterwards the grass looked as if a tank had driven across it!

It is worth making the point that you should always be prepared for a memorable shoot even when you do not expect it. Provision for carrying the bag back is essential and non-four-wheel drive vehicles cannot be expected to perform miracles. On this occasion, a real mess was made of the grass field. It turned out, fortunately, that it was due to be ploughed anyway, but say it had not been? There is a lesson here for everyone, and I have certainly learned from it.

May Shoot

I cannot be anecdotal about an early season shoot like this without giving an example of one which occurred late in the season, indeed very late since it was 18 May and most rape was well in flower. Spring drilling had passed and we had entered that quiet time which often follows it, when there may be little pigeon activity in some areas. I had been to look at a field of late drilled 'cuckoo corn' but found it to be attracting only a handful of scavenging rooks. The countryside was glowing in the spring sunshine and the lushness of growth and the variations of green gladdened the eye, which becomes so easily jaded by the drabness of our long northern winter.

I stopped to pass the field glasses over the fields of a farm which has been very productive down the years. The rape stood tall and was coming well into flower. I picked up pigeon movement along a line of willows at the far boundary of the rape. Then it became obvious that birds were pitching into the bottom corner. My investigations showed me that in this corner the rape was very immature indeed, having been grazed heavily in the winter, this being a well sheltered spot.

I made a natural hide in some bushes, put out a small pattern of decoys and was quickly into a very productive shoot which yielded close on a hundred birds. I had to cut my activities short because I was going out in the evening, otherwise I would certainly have been into a bag of well in excess of a hundred.

Seasonal Differences

The truth of rape shooting lies somewhere beyond the two anecdotes I have quoted. Large bags are difficult to make consistently and when they are, it is because the necessary ingredients for success, so to speak, have come together. The experience for most pigeon shooters is so frequently to be confronted with a huge flock of birds on a rape field, which all seems to promise a wonderful day. He then finds that the birds clear off *en masse* and do not return, or alternatively, they return once or twice in a big group, he has four or five shots and that is that.

Perhaps the main reason for this is that large congregations of winter pigeon tend to operate as one organism and in one sense lose their identity as individual birds. Their group instinct for survival drives them to stick together as a gang and so when disturbed they move as one and return or find another location as one body. Under certain conditions, as I said before, it makes them practically undecoyable. A strong wind though seems to make the birds more inclined to fly and move about, and appears to break up the tendency to flock. Birds then begin to move as individuals or in smaller parties and so become more of a decoyable proposition. Wind also tends to channel birds along more predictable lines so the odds shift more favourably in the decoyer's direction.

It becomes easier to make a shoot on rape as the spring comes on and the rape begins to grow. This is because the days lengthen and begin to warm up a little, so taking pressure off the birds. This causes more movement and feeding during the day. Earlier in the winter the birds tend to have two concentrated feeding spells, one very early and one later in the afternoon prior to going to roost. At the end of January I have seen birds which have returned to their roosting wood on the edge of a rape field, dropping down on the rape for a further feed when it has been practically dark – clearly not a decoyable proposition.

When the days warm up and the rape begins to grow the pigeons will really give the sweet new growth a hammering. How much they reduce the final yield is difficult to prove, but this is the time that many farmers feel that pigeons need to be kept off. Pigeons will also tend to go to for the less mature patches as the rape begins to get longer. This means that they are channelling to specific places and are that much more easy to decoy than when they are feeding over a wider area.

I have recorded over the years that my average bag per trip significantly increases as the year progresses, with a definite uplift on windy March days – bags have climbed more regularly at this time into the fifties and sixties, numbers rarely achieved in January.

Decoying on Rape

I have so often found that rape shooting has necessitated a number of changes in location during a day. Sometimes it will be several moves within a field and at other times a change of field itself. A bag of thirty or forty birds may have been shot in four different places. This is just the time when the mobility you gain by using net hides is really appreciated.

Farmers put out bale hides on rape but to be honest, apart from a very few occasions, I have rarely done any good from one. Pigeons seem to become suspicious of these hides and give them a wide berth if farmers have put banger guns by them. Although banger guns are often ineffective, it appears that when used with bale hides they can make the birds jumpy. I also find that bale hides are invariably put in the wrong spots, that is in places where the birds rarely feed instead of the sheltered hedgerow or warmer hollows. The odd time I have used a bale hide successfully it was placed almost in the hedge and was close to a well-favoured tree.

There was a time when I undertook very little in the way of lofting birds. It has appeared increasingly important in recent years to get some birds up where they can be seen from a distance. With the great acreages of rape grown this is especially important. I loft real birds using the frames I described earlier and have been well pleased with the results. Many full-bodied artificial decoys appear to increase in effectiveness when used as lofters in a tree, as opposed to being placed on the ground.

On the whole, I feel that it is useful to build up a good sized pattern of decoys when shooting over oil seed rape, since pigeon are expecting to see larger groups of birds feeding and anyway on big acreages a large pattern of birds is more noticeable.

It always appears to me that artificial decoys are less effective on oil seed rape than on some other crops and real birds, or derivatives from real birds, are much to be preferred. Every bird shot becomes a decoy and if artificials have been used to start the shoot they can be pulled in two at a time for each real bird set up. If a large number of artificials have been used in the first place, I would personally remove them at a higher rate. I do not really advocate mixing decoys though, either different types of artificial, or artificial and real. The days have gone when birds would come in to any old thing and I just do not feel that a mixture of types of decoy is effective. I do not mean by this that my real bird shells, when backed up by freshly shot birds, cease to be effective, since this is just the pattern I would favour.

I said before that winter shooting on oil seed rape can be frustrating and relatively unproductive. I hope the novice will see that there is a real challenge in making a bag and that sitting on any old rape field in a bale hide with twenty artificial decoys laid out is not a likely recipe for success. When people buy pigeon shooting over rape, this is often what they experience – no wonder they become dissatisfied and disillusioned.

Winter rape shooting can be hard, cold work, with little reward in terms of birds shot. It can, however, also be seen as refreshing, invigorating exercise which is a good deal better than being stuck in front of a television set or caught up with other milling thousands in some city shopping centre. Rape shooting can also be the way into more productive shooting later in the year, so it should be valued for the role it plays. There is always more to this sport than simply killing pigeons.

Rape can also produce some good shooting just before its harvest. Farmers may prepare oil seed rape for combining in two different ways. It may be sprayed with a chemical desiccant so that it dies off and ripens, enabling it to be combined direct, or it may be cut by machine and left in rows to ripen naturally – this is called swathe-rowing.

Swathe-rowed rape is what I am most interested in for shooting over in the summer, but first a word of caution. It is counter-productive for a pigeon shooter or his dog to go bashing about over the ripening rows, thereby shedding more seed than the pigeons are taking. Some farmers will allow no one near their rape at this stage and it is important to check and make sure that it is acceptable before setting up. I always restrict the use of my dog in this instance anyway.

Decoys can be set up on the rows and also dead birds can be set on frames to lift them into view of any birds which are passing. More often than not pigeons will be feeding all over the field and not just in one restricted spot. Finding the line is therefore important. As with winter shooting, wind is an asset. Birds may feed all day on the rape at this time but being high summer, activity builds up in the afternoon and early evening, so there is no need to be out at the crack of dawn.

I have found it helpful to shoot when the farmer has combined round the field a few times and then been held up for some reason, more often than not the weather. The bare area where the combine has passed is a useful spot on which to put the decoys and avoids the necessity of going into the rows, so long as the line of flight into the field has been located. Shooting over rape at this time is similar in fact to shooting over laid cereals, which I shall be dealing with in due course.

If the stubble is left after combining then birds may continue to glean any split seed off the field, and the shooting period is therefore further extended. A shower of rain will soon cause the loose seed which remains to germinate and it is not long before the field 'greens' up with sprouting seed. In its dicotyledon stage it is the mustard which school children grow on blotting paper in school. At this stage it is less attractive to the pigeons, who will be off to glean on laid cereals or other more productive stubbles.

6 Main Crops

Drilling

There is no doubt that for the pigeon shooter the cream of our sport coincides with the sowing of cereals, beans and peas. Of the two main drilling periods, spring drilling, in my book, has the edge over that undertaken in the autumn for productivity in terms of birds shot. Both periods have their own attractions and also their similarities. I would approach a shoot over spring drilling in a similar manner to one in autumn but I would probably have more confidence that the spring shoot would give me a larger bag.

During the early spring, pigeons will have been feeding almost exclusively on oil seed rape. The winter will have been long and rape will have figured as the staple diet for the birds. Grain and lentil (peas and beans) seed which they can glean from the sown fields are a welcome and nourishing change for the birds.

Not all birds leave the rape for the drilling and some shooters make a differentiation between what they call 'rape pigeon' and others. Some years I have gone from shooting birds on rape to drilling and back to rape again. Pigeons on drilling are gleaning the split seed which lies on the surface. They do not probe for seed and are not posing a threat to the crop. The justification for shooting them goes no further than the fact that their presence promises good sport which in turn means continuing control of numbers.

In the spring, besides sowings of wheat, barley and oats, there will also be peas and beans, both of which can prove a really attractive draw for the birds. In the spring of 1987 I took 186 pigeons from one drill-

ing in two consecutive afternoons, which proves the point.

I have read that some shooters nowadays experience a reticence by the birds to come right into the decoys. One experienced shot, writing in a sporting magazine, recently stated that he could not remember the last occasion when a pigeon actually landed amongst his decoys. It could well be that he lives in an area of the country where there is heavy pressure on the birds, or perhaps he should be looking at the effectiveness of his decoys, something I have done in a previous chapter. Certainly on both spring and autumn drilling, when using real birds or derivatives from real birds as decoys, I experience little reticence from my quarry. I should hasten to add that there are other occasions when I have encountered a certain shyness from the birds but I will deal with this in another section.

Not every sown field will produce a shoot. It may be a few days before birds 'switch on' to favoured fields anyway. It always appears to me that peas, for instance, become more attractive to pigeon when they have been rained on and this may well be because rain washes off the chemical with which they have been dressed.

The pressure is off the shooter in the spring, as he does not need to make a crack of dawn start – around eleven o'clock (or even twelve o'clock in late April) is usually the time when birds begin to flight. At this time of year birds will probably have fed at around six o'clock in the morning and have gone away to digest this first feed, returning later for a top-up.

The beauty of shooting over drilling lies in several factors. Drilling is generally much less taxing to walk on than some of the

Setting up a real bird as a decoy on drilling.

A wire frame can help make the first few real bird decoys you start off with look less flat and dead, by raising them slightly above the ground.

quagmires of the winter. Both spring and autumn often produce bright, windy days which have a classic rightness for decoying. All this certainly adds to the pleasantness of the activity but in practical terms, it must be said that decoys stand out very clearly on the bare soil of a sown field and, providing the pattern looks convincing, the birds will oblige more readily than they were prepared to do on the winter rape.

In spring, birds are operating more individually, or at least in smaller groups than in winter, making them far easier to decoy. In autumn, however, there can be gangs of young birds around which operate in fairly large flocks and can sometimes behave in a manner more familiar to the 'big flocks on rape' syndrome. I encountered something of this over bean stubble in late October in 1987, but as it was a later season, drilling was still going on in November and by then I was encountering the flock syndrome less.

One factor which can make autumn drilling less productive than that of the spring depends on what sort of acorn year it has been. When the woodland oaks have produced a good acorn yield, pigeon will often prefer to glean these than visit farmland for food. When this occurs then the pigeon shooter is going to have a more disappointing time of it than normal.

Autumn-sown cereals have a higher yield than those sown in the spring and consequently farmers work all out in the back end of the year to drill as much as they can before the weather closes in. The consequence of this is that there is less acreage of drilling around in the spring to attract birds, so they tend to concentrate more on the really attractive sowings at that time.

Spring drilling follows a period when the birds have really only had rape to sustain them, whereas the autumn drilling coincides with a time of abundant natural fruits and follows close on the heels of harvest. Therein lies the basic difference.

Although spring days are generally more productive, autumn days can have, for me,

the more special feel. There is a particularly good feeling about a classic autumn day when the trees and hedgerows are burnished golden and the air carries a hint of winter. Autumn light has a mellow quality which adds a special charm to the countryside for those with an appreciative eye for the aesthetic, which I hope is most of us.

Productive Shoots

It is so easy when recalling pigeon shoots to write about the really productive ones and to ignore the less successful. I think anyone writing about the sport should be mindful of the need *not* to imply to the less experienced that a bag of, say, a hundred birds is attainable all that often under prevailing modern conditions. I average 32 birds per trip. If I was to average my shoots solely over spring drilling then the number climbs to 65. I must, however, include those winter days when six in the bag is all I have to show for my efforts, hence the lower figure.

There are shooters who will not shoot over rape because of its inherent difficulties. I have to say that I have little time for those who will not take the rough with the smooth. There is little justice in a sport in which you can defend a farmer's rape through the slush and mud of winter, only to find that a fair-weather pigeon shooter pops up around Easter and beats you to one or two really fantastic shoots over the peas. To be fair this is a sport for the opportunist and you should not be too peeved if an opportunist gunner beats you to it, aggravating though it is.

I remember a couple of years ago, taking an acquaintance pigeon shooting very close to Easter. Spring was beginning to paint the hedgerows with a pastel green and there was a subtle difference in the air from only a week or two before. My partner and I set up on a rape field belonging to a large estate where I have had good sport down the years. The extensive woodlands round us glowed in the sun, which was beginning to show a little warmth. A light breeze stirred the grasses in the hedgerow as we waited for a return of the pigeons we had seen feeding there.

They did in fact oblige and shooting was quite good, but by 1.30 p.m. everything tailed off and there was that feeling in the air that nothing else was going to happen. We collected our modest bag of 37 birds and headed for a quick pint. Suitably refreshed I suggested to my companion that we take a ride across my area. We had had a reasonable session and everything else we might pick up would be a bonus. Bob agreed that this was a good idea so we set off in a fairly relaxed mood.

There was comparatively little drilling that year since the back-end of the previous year had been particularly good and farmers had achieved a high acreage of drilling in the fine October weather. This following spring had found the rape particularly productive. As I have said, it was around Easter time, which was well into April that year, and we had had an above average shoot off the rape already that day.

We had travelled no more than about three miles after leaving the pub when we spotted a fairly small field which was absolutely alive with pigeon. Pigeon shooting writers love to use the expression 'blue with pigeon' but, to be honest, pigeon working a drilling in either spring or autumn sunshine always look white to me. Perhaps I should start a new trend and say that this field was absolutely white with birds! The line of approach was easy to see. Two fields away behind our field stood, and indeed still stands, a block of woodland from which a steady trickle of birds were heading and pitching in to feed.

Bob and I almost ran across the drilling, which was sown with peas. We set up near the only resting tree in the far hedge. The wind was in our backs and 15 birds from our morning's shoot made an effective pattern to our front. Amongst the decoys I placed some flutterers. To be honest, I just made that name up for want of a better one. This means of presenting a dead bird decoy is achieved by simply cutting a slender stick from the hedgerow, which is then pushed via the bird's vent right through to the head. The stick is then set into the ground at a 45 degree angle with the bird facing into the wind. The wing bones of the bird are snapped close to the shoulder (if fingers are not strong enough then use pliers). Two thin sticks are then split in the top and placed either side of the bird, the wings stretched out and the tip of each wing slotted into the split stick.

The wind will cause this real bird decoy to flutter and move in a realistic manner and will prove a really effective pigeon puller, under the right conditions. A word of caution though – when the conditions are very still, this type of decoy with outspread wings may well turn birds which would otherwise come into the decoys.

The April day I am recalling was quite breezy and the decoys, both static and those designed for movement, proved effective, borne out by the fact that Bob and I picked up a further 76 birds by close of play, which came at around six o'clock in the evening.

I could profitably make the point here that the modern pigeon shooter must be a real opportunist, flexible in his approach, and prepared to be mobile to find his sport. This day, a bag of 113 pigeons was built by operating on two separate crops in two different locations. I could add that on occasions I have moved four times to make a bag of 30 birds. The whole point is that there are times when you must trust your judgement as to whether a move is likely to be more profitable than to stay put. If Bob and I had stayed on the rape that would probably only have achieved a long period of inactivity followed by a flurry of movement of birds in the late afternoon, and possibly a total bag of 50 or 60. Not a totally unacceptable quantity you might say, but I must comment that the day we

A means of displaying a dead bird which the author describes as a flutterer.

experienced remains in my memory because of the way it was structured, whereas many 50–60 bag days over rape have individually long been forgotten.

By way of a postscript to this story. I later discovered that one of the 'fair weather brigade' had taken 189 birds off that very field the day before. The day after my shoot he took a further 69 and another chap a further 30 or so.

Travelling Light

My shooting partner, Doug, and I often start out in the same hide together, and when we see how the birds are reacting then one of us sets off to find another spot which will hopefully profit the both of us. We used this tactic recently to good advantage on a huge field of 130 acres. The field had beans on it that year and the farmer has since drilled with winter wheat.

The vagaries of this particular season have put certain demands on farmers and such has been the case in this instance. The field was, by necessity, ploughed, worked and drilled in successive strips as the weather would allow. It had proved a very good pigeon draw over quite an extended period. It is a strange field, as large as many small farms. It slopes steeply uphill from one boundary which consists of a tall, thick hedge full of mature oaks and then falls in a long sweep away from the middle down to a brook which is sparsely lined with bushes.

Doug and I set up in the oak-lined hedge after seeing a large number of birds feeding on the sheltered bank. A good flight of in-coming birds was an encouraging sight. Our shoot started well enough but we seemed to be pushing the birds over the ridge and the action became slower. It became obvious that we needed to split up so I set off with my dog Sam, gun, cart-ridges, one short piece of net and four dead birds.

I really love these 'travelling light' soli-tary sorties and Doug and I have frequently employed them to good advantage under the right conditions. As I cleared the ridge I could see where our birds had gone, since the margin of the brook was lined with a huge number of pigeon feeding totally un-disturbed and too far off to be stirred by our shots from the far side of this great expanse of prairie.

Cover was poor along the brook but about 150 yards from it, a spur of hedgerow jutted out from the boundary hedge at that end of the field. I set out my little flock of four birds, made a small hollow in the thick hedge and draped my little piece of net across the gap. From the outside it was impossible to see any sign of a hide. A further advantage of this hide lay in the fact that overhead cover was total and no high flying birds could possibly look in on me.

I had scarcely climbed into cover when there were birds milling everywhere. They were in the air and landing on the drilling, some literally seven or eight yards from me. I managed to shoot one on the ground and

missed a departing bird with a hurried shot. A large group of birds like this can so often make one indecisive as to which individual bird to choose. When this happens it is so easy to miss what should have been a straightforward shot.

It was a beautiful day. The sun shone and the sky was blue. The last leaves of autumn glowed red and yellow on hedge and tree and I fancied that there was nowhere in time or place that I would rather be than that corner of an English field on a golden autumn afternoon.

There was a good strong wind blowing directly from behind me and this caused the birds to come straight towards me. I found that I was taking one bird head-on and then the second barrel would be at either a bird twisting away to get the wind behind it or at a bird pushing on past me up the field. The wind brought the occasional 'pop! pop!' and I was pleased that our strategy

Natural cover and a piece of net makes a quick and effective hide, easy to construct.

was working and that birds were now being pushed back to Doug.

All too quickly the afternoon sun mellowed and dipped; shadows began to lengthen and my supply of birds trickled away. I collected the slain and hung them on the game carriers which I always carry in my game pocket. Then dog and I slogged back up the slope to collect Doug, a load of 51 pigeons adding to the exertion caused by the uneven surface of the land and the long drag up to the ridge.

I topped the rise and could see no sign of my friend, but then a whistle carried from far off and I could see him back at the car. It is uncanny how we always seem to know simultaneously when the hour has come to call it a day. We have talked about this and we both say that you feel when a shoot has ended and it is time to make tracks. This derives from experience gained from other shoots and other times I suppose.

I tried this field the following week. Drilling had moved a further strip over and birds were still there in quantity. It was a damp misty day which threatened but never quite came to rain. By half past one the light had faded to what you would normally expect in the late afternoon and there was a 'dead' feel about the day. The whole atmosphere was one of pessimism for my chances and I longed for that welcome ingredient, a good wind, to get up – but no such luck! I know when conditions have beaten me and I retreated for home with just six birds.

Missed Opportunities

Taking opportunities when they present themselves is what this shooting game is about. 'Strike while the iron is hot' is an adage worth believing in. To show you the truth of this and to illustrate that pigeon shooting can often produce its missed chances, let me relate the following experience.

The phone rang one evening and I discovered that I was speaking to a young man who was a keen pigeon shooter but who had never made a large bag at decoying, despite the fact that he worked on a large farm in North Bedfordshire which attracted large quantities of pigeon. My young acquaintance went on to say that the drilling of 40 acres of beans was imminent on his employer's farm and would I like to join him in an attempt to decoy any pigeon which might decide these beans were to their liking. My answer was in the affirmative and I advised my informant that he should watch the field and contact me at the first sign of pigeon activity.

Several weeks passed but no word came and I assumed that the prospects in Bedfordshire had not come up to expectation. Then one evening the phone rang again – the beans had been drilled and could I make it on Saturday? One small problem had transpired, though, in the form of another pigeon shooter who had gained permission to shoot the beans a day or so previously. This shooter, by all accounts, had given the birds something of a hammering. It was the classic case of our golden opportunity falling to someone else's opportunism.

The other shooter had put in a very full day, firing over 600 cartridges and picking up a bag of 219 pigeon. This I knew did not bode well for our chances but being ever the optimist I met my young friend on the Saturday as arranged.

Conditions could not have been better, since it was clear, with a stiff wind blowing. A few birds rose on our approach, which was slightly encouraging, but I noticed that the beans had sprouted and were well through the soil, which to my mind immediately puts paid to their attractiveness.

To cut a long story short, we shot six birds. The 750 cartridges that I had taken to Bedfordshire proved definitely surplus to requirements.

Peas

If oil seed rape is frequently the bane of the pigeon decoyer's life, then peas are often his salvation. Peas are drilled in the spring and pigeon find them a magnetic draw once they have discovered the field. It sometimes appears that a shower of rain is required to make the peas more attractive to the birds. It may well be that this is so since peas are dressed with chemical and a shower possibly washes some of this off and makes the seed more palatable for the birds.

Pigeon working a pea drilling are gleaning scattered surface seed and are not really a threat to the crop at this stage. Most farmers, however, do not want the birds to get into the habit of seeking a meal on their pea fields since once the crop begins to germinate and sprout, pigeons will continue to find them very much to their liking.

Peas will attract pigeon from drilling right through their growing period to their harvest. Even after harvest the stubble will often continue to attract birds and provide sport. It is small wonder therefore that I view this crop as an important producer of sport since it will provide me with shooting from April to September.

I tackle the task on freshly drilled peas in the same manner as I would any shoot over drilling; however, when the peas begin to grow then there is a need to lift the decoys to a visible height. Frames for mounting real birds are useful at this stage as are frames for lofting birds on well-used trees.

It is frequently stated by pigeon shooters that the more decoys you put out the better. Generally speaking this may be true but it is not always the case. I have frequently noticed on growing peas that once I have built up a decoy pattern beyond a dozen or so birds, incoming pigeon seem deterred by my artificial flock, yet when I have reduced the numbers displayed, the birds resumed coming in confidently. I believe that there are certain circumstances prevailing when pigeon do not *expect* to see a large company of their own kind and a very big pattern of decoys can be counter-productive. I have discussed this with other pigeon shooters expecting to be pooh-poohed but have been heartened that others have experienced this also. To be honest it may not have as much to do with the number of birds set up as decoys, as with their density. The explanation for this probably lies in the fact that birds feeding in the late spring are acting as individuals, pairs, or very small groups, and not as big, single-minded flocks. There may be a large congregation of birds on a field of peas but it has been built up in the manner described and is spread out over a large area. If you watch a pea field in late May or June you will often notice, unless a strong wind is blowing, that birds are dropping all over the crop and not necessarily in one concentrated spot.

During the late spring and early summer although birds may have been working the peas all day, it is usually in the afternoon and evening that feeding activity hots up. Prior to harvest it may possibly be late afternoon before a flight switches on in a truly productive sense.

A year or two ago, I had scouted my area all day for a potential shoot but had failed to spot anything worth while. About halfway through the afternoon I met a young farmer who provided me with the information that one of his father's pea fields had a very sparse crop on it and that it had recently been pulling quite a few pigeon. I had two of my young sons with me and I think that they had assumed that pigeon shooting consisted merely of picnics and chats to farmers since our day so far had produced only that.

I found the pea field as directed and discovered that birds were working the whole extent of it. I made a hide close to a tree and decided to give some light plastic shell decoys I was carrying a good field test. The crop was indeed very sparse but I thought that the farmer's loss was my gain since my decoys would be easier for the birds to spot.

The shell decoys seemed to glint and shine unnaturally in the sun but I wanted to give them a reasonable trial so I left them out. It was probably around 3.30 p.m. when I shot my first pigeon. I left all the birds where they fell and set none whatsoever as decoys. The only birds I retrieved were either winged or had dropped on the grass behind me. I carried 89 birds off the field that evening. Success on this scale was due, I believe, to two factors: there was a wind (and wind is always good news), and birds were really keen on that field, making it a natural hot spot.

When I shot this field a few days later I tried my artificial shells again but birds would not come within range – I had to replace them with my home-made shell decoys before the birds would play ball. I shot 42 birds during the course of the afternoon – clearly an acceptable bag – but this field was no longer quite the hot spot it had been, at least not under the conditions which prevailed when I was free to visit it, until it was eventually harvested.

Laid Cereals

Early summer storms often flatten large areas of cereals and these provide pigeons with the opportunity to feed on ripening grain. Even small patches of laid cereals will attract pigeon, although these smaller areas may not be so convenient to shoot over. It is worth watching out for laid corn, as pigeon shooters refer to flattened cereals, from mid-June onwards. Winter barley may provide the first draw but wheat when still unripe and 'milky' is also very attractive to the birds.

The season for shooting over laid cereals may extend from June to August depending upon the year. As with summer crops, some birds will be coming and going most of the day, but the afternoon and evening will see most activity, particularly during the hotter days of mid-summer onwards.

I prefer the larger flattened areas of cereals on which to decoy for one main reason. If I shoot pigeon, it gives me no satisfaction to drop them where they are irretrievable. However good a shot you may be, it can prove extremely difficult to kill birds consistently over even a reasonably large flat patch. Birds which fall in the standing crop must be considered lost, since no farmer is going to be overjoyed by the sight of a pigeon shooter wallowing about doing more damage than he is worth in terms of prevention.

I believe that the quality of my decoys and their visibility to the quarry is more important than quantity. Packing an available area of laid corn with decoys is not usually the answer to building a successful shoot. If passing pigeon see that there is little room left as a potential landing space they will show little inclination to come in close enough to be shootable. The answer is to space your decoys well and to leave a clear landing area which may well also become a killing area as the shoot gets going. Frames to lift decoys above the level of the surrounding crop can also prove valuable.

A ploy which I value when shooting on cereals is to see if there are any trees under which there is a flattened area. Decoys lofted on the outside branches of the tree, despite the fact that it is in full leaf, will be quite easily spotted by the birds and they will be drawn to them. If you discipline yourself to shooting only at the birds coming to the tree, it will be found that nearly all the birds shot will be easily retrieved. I would much rather shoot 30 birds this way and take them all home than treble the number and pick a quarter of them.

Stubbles

I have seldom found the early stubbles all that productive for pigeon shooting locally.

It has been my experience that foraging birds are more inclined to seek laid corn areas than to utilise the stubbles. I am ready to accept, however, that in other areas stubble figures more importantly as a pigeon lure than it does here on my own patch before all combining has taken place.

Nowadays the speed of harvest and consequent cultivation of the land means that most stubbles are quickly turned under and few usually remain until that period when they would really come into their own, which is just prior to, or coinciding with, autumn drilling. A difficult year, such as 1987, spreads harvest over a long period and stubbles are therefore around much longer than usual. Bean stubble of course provides useful shooting in the autumn because beans are always the last crop to be combined. This year I am still getting productive shoots off them and it is early December, which can so often be a frustratingly hungry gap from the shooter's point of view, before we begin on the inevitable rape.

Whether it has been a cereal, rape, pea or bean stubble, I have found that productive shoots off them have generally been from September onwards. On occasion a good shoot on stubble has coincided with a shoot on drilling all on the same day and on the same farm. An autumn day which exemplifies this happened a year or two ago when my friend Doug and I visited one of my most valued farms.

It was a bright, windy afternoon in mid-October and we discovered a great many birds working two adjacent bean stubbles. There was one spot which appeared to be the place and right under the main flight too. We decided to share a hide and had expectations of a reasonable shoot. All the elements were there to make us optimistic.

The ideal situation for most of us is to find a good location where the birds will play ball, keep coming and a bag is made with relatively little effort. On this afternoon our feelings were, as I said, optimistic

because of the presence of a large number of birds, an incoming flight taking place, and a good stiff breeze to help keep things lively.

We shot a few birds but the action was not as swift as we had hoped. We soon noticed that a steady stream of birds were following a line of trees bordering a brook at the bottom end of our field so I left Doug with sole ownership of the hide and set off with gun, cartridges, a tiny piece of camouflage netting and three dead birds to see if I could find another spot which might prove more beneficial for my partner and myself.

My wanderings that afternoon led me down the field and over and along the brook. The birds were flighting along the brook and I could see that some were pitching on to the drilling close by the margin. I needed to expend little energy by way of preparation as natural cover was abundant. I placed my dead birds out on the drilling and waited confidently. Within seconds I shot my first and only customer and that was that. Other birds continued to pass by, 70–80 yards out and totally ignoring my little group of decoys which were now of course increased to four.

To sit it out was pointless so off I set again, this time much further along the hedge to where quite a number of birds rose from a dip in the ground. My immediate thought was to blame myself for not realising that the birds would be using the sheltered spots on a day like this. I set up again but I am afraid to say that I had read the signs incorrectly again since absolutely nothing came in to my decoys. I did notice, however, that the boundary hedge which lay at a right angle running up from the brook had birds crossing regularly about 150 yards up it.

Now this is the very hedge where I had had such a marvellous shoot several years before when the field behind had been rape and I had subsequently got stuck when taking my car over the grass to collect the bag. What was to follow was in a way a repeat performance of that memorable day, but

Setting out shell decoys on bean stubble. Note the Richardson Rocker.

with a different draw for the birds and two months difference in the season.

I went at a trot to where the birds were crossing the hedge and realised for the first time that the pigeons were being drawn to the field behind by a cereal stubble which had been allowed to linger a little later than is usual on this farm. My reconnaissance was clearly to blame. Doug and I had been attracted too quickly and easily to what we had expected to be a hot spot, that is the bean stubble, and not really investigated further what was happening round and about. If you had asked me the order of attractive feeding for the birds I would have said bean stubble, drilling, followed by the maturing cereal stubble. That's what *I* would have said, but no one had asked the birds. They were actually indicating that cereal stubble, then bean stubble and the drilling, just to rest on, was the order of preference.

Aided by a very shallow ditch, my little piece of net and whatever bits and pieces of natural foliage I could find, I made a barely adequate and extremely uncomfortable hide, and waited to see if it would be third time lucky. I placed three of my decoys in a feeding position out on the drilling and the other one was set up with a stick through the vent, wings extended. This decoy I think proved an irresistible draw, fluttering in the wind as it did.

Birds began to swoop in before I had time to even get in the hide. Twenty-five cartridges were fired as quickly as the gun could be loaded. Then there was a lull. This quiet period was followed by a stream of customers which came in a steady, if somewhat less dramatic, fashion.

When all action had drawn to a close and the shadows began to lengthen in the early evening sunshine, I picked up the slain and strung the birds on to my indispensable shoulder game carriers. It was a reasonably straightforward downhill slog to the car. It is at times like this when I am glad that I have travelled light and that the heaviest burden has been caused by a successful shoot by any standards!

When I reached the farm roadway I was mighty pleased to see Doug, face flushed with pleasure having experienced success on a similar scale, coming along with the car, so saving me a further hike. My partner had benefited by my stirring of the birds. He had shot on the bean stubble; I had been shooting on drilling although the real draw had been the cereal stubble. Doug had spent a sedentary afternoon; I had had a physically exerting time of it. The whole episode just goes to show the satisfaction to be gained from this do-it-yourself sport, in terms that typify its true hunting appeal.

I cannot let pass at this juncture the opportunity to describe a shoot which happened in a similar manner not long ago when my teenage son accompanied me in the hopes of a reasonable day's shooting. Jeremy and I were just unloading our gear from the car, intent on tackling a bean stubble, which had been attracting an enormous number of birds, when the farmer arrived to plough it. It is not a large field, so the presence of the farmer proved to be far too disruptive for a good shoot to be contemplated – although this can sometimes still happen on the larger, prairie-type fields, despite ongoing cultivations. Besides we also had the safety feature to consider.

Jeremy and I moved further along the high lane above the field and barely half a mile away we could see a promising number of birds streaming over a ploughed field towards a cereal stubble. Had we found another hot spot? We set our hide on the ploughed side and put our decoys on the furrows where they showed up beautifully plainly. The birds poured in and Jeremy, sharing my hide and using a very light side-by-side twelve bore of mine, downed 19 very sporting birds on the wing. The lad was disappointed not to make an even 20 but such is pigeon shooting. We did, however, carry a joint bag of 93 pigeon off the field that evening.

I do not wish to convey the impression that large bags like this are the norm. I relate these examples to illustrate the potential productiveness of a particular crop or ground cover, especially when ideal weather conditions prevail.

Alternative Crops

The main venues for the decoyer are, as I have illustrated, rape, drilling, peas, laid cereals and stubbles. These crops tend to occupy the thinking of those of us who operate very largely in these main arable areas, where pigeon numbers are at their highest concentrations. These are not the only crops which will attract pigeon, for apart from a variety of natural fruits, the birds will also take clover, brassica crops, field lupins in the early stage of growth, seedlings of certain root crops, soft fruits and sheep turnips. It is really down to the individual shooter to know the cropping patterns within his own area and to ascertain those crops which are attracting sufficient birds to give him a shoot.

I have made only a few shoots on clover over the past few years and they were not spectacular. I have not seen any lucerne grown since the 1960s when it was a good draw for pigeon. Kale has given me some good shooting when the birds have been forced to leave the rape because of deep snow. To be honest, though, they often manage to graze the rape however deep the precipitation since the wind always exposes areas of the crop sufficiently to sustain the birds. We seem to come round to that stuff rape time and time again don't we? Well, we are bound to, considering how it has come to dominate the arable scene over so much of the United Kingdom. It seems to me,

incidentally, that rape must be very nourishing for the birds for I very rarely shoot razor-breasted birds, even after a prolonged cold spell, unlike years ago when birds went very thin after even a short cold spell.

Fodder rape in June can produce some good shooting late in the afternoon or early evening. A few years ago my neighbour's son came to report that he had seen birds flighting to a field of fodder rape when returning home on the school bus. I went to investigate and discovered that quite a few birds were flighting from nearby woodland to this field. It was on a farm which was not within my shooting domain so I sought permission and had to wait two days for a phone call granting my request as the farmer had been away.

The day I arrived to shoot this field was very windy, indeed an almost gale force wind prevailed. I made a hide from elder branches which I found difficult to keep in place. In fact by the end of the shoot I had just one branch left in position.

The birds came battling low up in the field against the wind and on each occasion they came after the first shot, they let themselves be torn away like leaves on the wind making a second shot extremely difficult. Between half past six and eight o'clock, I shot 28 birds. I had an extremely entertaining evening and although by some standards not large, a bag such as this was to me quite satisfactory.

I did not achieve another shoot on this field for boisterous summer storms, which that evening's high wind had preceded, flattened large areas of surrounding cereals and the birds switched their attentions to these. Keeping your eyes open, watching the birds' behaviour and being awake to local cropping, is always the key to success.

7 Roost Shooting and Flighting

Roost Shooting

I have spent many happy hours waiting for pigeon to return to their roosting woods. It is one of those activities which can be undertaken alone, with one or two friends, or as part of an organised exercise to control pigeon numbers, when a large number of shooters may be involved.

There is something special about being in the woods on an evening in winter or early spring. As you wait patiently for the first birds to appear, an air of expectancy seems to fill the air. The fading light and the sounds of the wood gradually becoming hushed add to the feeling of anticipation.

I love the woods in all their moods. Sometimes there is snow lying, making the trees black and skeletal against a grey and lowering sky, or at other times spring is in the air and snowdrops brighten the woodland floor. To anyone with a degree of sensitivity, it is all equally pleasurable, for the smell and sensations of woodland are special whatever the season.

It has been my experience that I shoot a larger quantity of pigeon when there are sufficient guns in the woods to keep them on the move. My most enjoyable shoots, though, have been on those occasions when I have been totally alone.

I seem to have things to myself when there is snow. I love snow, in moderation, and a fall is enough to motivate me into action and send me heading for those woodlands to which I have access. If decoying activities have been suspended during the day because of snow and I have been house-bound, then around mid-afternoon, both dog and I become decidedly 'twitchy'. It is then that the anticipation of going roost shooting has its greatest effect and appeal.

Whatever the prevailing weather conditions there is no doubt that wind is a desirable factor in roost shooting, as it is for all pigeon shooting. It always amazes me how the wind can be positively roaring in the tops of the trees, which are swaying madly and the whole wood can be full of creaks and groans, yet there is a feeling of calm at ground level.

A high wind brings pigeons over the trees at a reasonable shooting height, although it is true that at the sound of a shot they will be tossed quickly away like leaves on the wind, making a second barrel difficult. When there is little wind and conditions are calm, pigeon come in over the woods at almost stratospheric levels and can be out of shot for most waiting guns.

Solitary Shoots

Roost shooting alone is slightly different from shooting in company. It is usually difficult, when you are alone, to build a comparatively large bag of birds, since surrounding woodland is left undisturbed and birds which you have saluted are going to be able to find an alternative haven which is both quiet and safer in which to roost. If I get into double figures when shooting alone, then I feel that I have done really well. Some fortunate shooters may have access to woodland where the birds literally pour in in large numbers, and quite large bags are possible, even to a solitary gun. This is not my experience and probably not that of many like me. I will always make the point though that in the end, the size of the bag, if not a total irrelevancy, is certainly not the overriding consideration.

Some years ago I had access to a series of spinneys which crown a low ridge of hills not far from where I live. I was indeed privileged to have permission to shoot there, for no one else had – the spinneys were, and still are, a haven for foxes. The owner is a hunting man of some repute and his paramount interest lies in making sure that his foxes remain undisturbed. Nonetheless, I had managed to gain access to this lovely area. Adjoining these spinneys was a further area of narrow woodland which was approached through the grounds of a large, untenanted, country house, and I often used to park my car in its courtyard.

As I was the only shooter to frequent the woods, my bags were seldom large and I often wished for someone else to be ensconced in the far end of the woods to keep the birds moving. Despite the smallish bags, many memorable evenings were spent there and one in particular sums up all I feel about roost shooting.

It had been a day of prolonged and heavy snow. Decoying was off the agenda and Sam and I had spent a leisurely day at home. Around three o'clock in the afternoon the snow had eased and I mentioned to my wife that I was considering a ride over to the spinneys. Needless to say, she suggested that I had taken leave of my senses but I was not to be swayed and, suitably attired in waxproof suit, loaded the dog and set off.

The main road was reasonably clear although rutted snow clanked ominously against the car's exhaust. When I turned off the main road on to the lane which led to the hills, I found it to be a virgin expanse of white snow but fortunately with no drifting. The long driveway down to the old house was a picture; a long ribbon of unbroken snow lined with snow-clad

conifers, a Christmas card scene so often unseen in my part of England at Christmas but frequently witnessed in early January, as indeed it so happened to be.

I parked the car as usual and walked across a small paddock to the first spinney. A few yards into the wood stood an aged ash tree, almost entirely clad in ivy. At the base was a hollow, affording a sheltered haven from the wind which was venomously scouring the ridge. As I waited, with Sam shivering, more from anticipation than the biting cold, a light powdering of snow began to fall and the wind strengthened. The old tree groaned, the wind boomed in the high tops overhead and bare branches clashed like fighting staves in the wood as the powdery snow sizzled through the twigs. It is at times like this that my senses are heightened and I feel truly alive.

I had my back to the bole of the tree, the wind coming from behind me. Pigeons will often come on the wind but then turn and pitch in against it. I expected birds over my location because in the sheltered hollows of the spinney behind me lay a belt of conifers and other evergreens, making the place a reasonably warm roost.

The pigeons came swirling on the wind, crops distended with oil seed rape that, despite the snowbound fields, they had still managed to graze. I enjoyed some brisk shooting. The dog did sterling work as the wind carried some birds which had fallen to my shot, way down the slope from my position.

It all ended suddenly. Darkness had stolen quickly over us and the light had rapidly decayed, as it does at this time of year. Besides, the snow now had all the signs of becoming a 'white out'. I had nine birds to hand and one stuck irretrievably in the ivy fastness above my head.

I made my contented way back through the paddock, up through the terraced garden into the courtyard. The dark, curtainless windows of the old house stared at me, black and empty. I felt uneasy and only briefly returned their gaze, childishly anxious and feeling that to stare longer would cause some awful apparition to appear, framed there in one of those uncurtained spaces. Today, the old house has new tenants and light now glows in those once uninviting windows. The spinneys still stand, invitingly close to home but I have other woods to tread and have not been in my old haunt for some time. Nonetheless, the memories are fresh and easily rekindled, for such is the lasting appeal of our sport.

Organised Trips

Besides the solitary excursion which may be savoured like the sipping of malt whisky, there is great enjoyment to be gained from the organised roost shoot. This can perhaps be likened more to the *bonhomie* of a drinking session in the pub with the lads, which of course may often follow a roost shooting session in company anyway.

Gun clubs, wild fowling associations and groups of farmers are the main organisers of large scale roost shoots. Obviously you need to be the invited guest of a member to be included on a club shoot. Sometimes roost shoots organised by local farming groups and designed as a pigeon control exercise, are advertised in the local press. I have seen such events organised by Rotary clubs, perhaps with a £5 subscription payable and the proceeds going to charity. Anyone desperate for pigeon shooting could well be vigilant to the possibility of obtaining at least some shooting in this way.

If shooting is going to be done in an organised way, it is useful to be mindful of a number of ground rules. If you have a dog, always ascertain beforehand whether or not you will be permitted to take it with you. A dog is a great asset, as I have said in a previous chapter, but not everyone is going to welcome a large gang of hopeful pigeon shooters, accompanied by assorted canines of dubious quality as biddable gun dogs. Many estates, whilst allowing periodical roost shooting, will adamantly say no to dogs.

On organised shoots there is, or at least should be, someone in overall control. It may be a keeper, club or syndicate official. This person will, or again, *should* lay down the basic principles by which the shoot is to be conducted.

When a large number of people are loose in the woods then the first consideration must be safety. The shooting of ground game, that is rabbits, must be taboo, as is any low elevation shooting, whether at pigeon or not. The old adage, 'never shoot where you can't see' is absolutely correct. You may feel you are the only one in a large section of woodland but other shooters may have been tempted to move from their own stations and have encroached into your area without your knowledge; this is why safety must come first.

The shoot organiser should tell everyone to stay in their block of woodland anyway. Safety considerations apart, it can be frustrating to have the makings of a shoot and then find that someone has muscled into your area and cut the birds' line, so depriving you of sport. This has happened to me on more than one occasion and can prove very annoying. Besides, when a shooter has moved from his piece of woodland, you can bet that pigeon will settle there undisturbed, so if the person to whom the area was allocated had just been a little more patient, he would have had some shooting anyway. It is always a case of the luck of the draw. One week you may be placed in a real hot spot and on another occasion it may be a dead loss; however, this is pot luck and must be put up with.

A shoot leader will always tell the guns the time when shooting must cease. This must be strictly adhered to, for to do otherwise may disturb pheasants coming into roost and antagonise the keeper, thereby jeopardising future pigeon shooting in those woods.

I always feel encouraged when I hear shoot organisers ask everyone to refrain from shooting at very high and speculative birds. A still, calm evening will probably find the birds coming in very high, and effectively out of range of guns placed on the periphery of a wood. This often does not deter certain over-exuberant types from blasting off at them. This may result in unnecessary wounding which is unsporting and inhumane; it is also selfish. It is always better to let high birds drop to the optimum height for the guns stationed further in the wood, then as the birds streak away they will provide other people with a more shootable, although undoubtedly very testing, target. I have seen very high birds, which have been saluted by enthusiastic guns on the periphery of the roosting wood, merely swing away and drift to woodland halfway to the next county, from where they are not going to return that evening.

An experienced roost shooter will always have a little scout round the piece of wood he has been allocated, being careful, as I said before, not to encroach upon anyone else's spot. If any trees are found which are well splashed with droppings and there are further droppings and feathers on the woodland floor, it may be assumed that this is, or at least has been, a favoured roosting spot and is worth covering.

Cover

I try to find a location with a few spaces in the canopy of twigs overhead, as too many thick and intertwined branches can stop the passage of your shot, as well as being very offputting. If there is some cover in the way of rhododendron or laurel, then I make use of it, since our sharp-sighted quarry may well detect the unbroken form of a pigeon shooter and turn before coming within range. If there is not suitable cover then I merely position myself close in against the trunk of a tree and remain still. This is often

When roost shooting, position yourself against the trunk of a tree . . .

103

. . . or use available cover.

Lofting a real bird decoy.

sufficient and makes the shooter quite un-obtrusive to incoming birds.

With the development of lightweight netting, a piece of camouflage can now be easily carried in the pocket to be suspended from lower branches so as to act as a screen from behind which to shoot. One large wood in which I shoot has some very tall trees but a very open woodland floor, and I always make sure that I have a piece of net with me to create some cover.

Some keen roost shooters will place lofted decoys in the trees, even leaving them there semi-permanently. I cannot be bothered with this sort of thing, being basically lazy I suppose. There are, how-ever, a number of instances when I might use decoys.

There is a spur of woodland which juts out into the neighbouring arable prairie and which is usually a good spot from which to bag a few home-bound pigeon. A small quantity of pigeon actually roost in this narrow salient of trees but it also forms part of a well-established line which pigeons use as a route to other deeper woods.

If I have been decoying locally, and the afternoon's activities have tailed off, then I will often head for this spur of wood in good time before roost, armed with perhaps eight or ten dead birds. These birds I set up on the field outside the wood – exactly where will depend upon the wind. I have so often found that early birds will make an attempt to come into my little pattern, but, more importantly, the decoys have the effect of just pulling the bigger, home-bound groups of birds over my position. It is, I suppose, a cross between decoying and roost shooting and can produce, when con-ditions are right and the birds are there, a simulation of driven pheasant shooting in woodland.

Skill

There is undoubtedly much skill in shoot-ing birds seen through a lace-work of twigs and branches. I would advise anyone shooting under conditions where the sky is cluttered with woodwork in this way to ignore it. Certainly, it is sensible to avoid spots which have too many close, thick branches, if possible. It is also useful if there are gaps, but if there are not it does not mean to say that the birds passing over are unshootable. When I used to shoot pigeon in the woods with a .22 rifle, one twig in the way would deflect the bullet from its mark. Twigs may do some damage to a shotgun cartridge's pattern of shot, but will usually not detract from its lethal quality.

Most shooters who cannot shoot consis-tently well in woodland but are otherwise competent shots, are usually hesitant and tentative in firing at presentable targets. They will probably also be checking the swing of the gun through the target – something which will most likely be un-consciously done, and which is caused by being too aware of the supposed overhead obstructions. Forgetting about these obstructions and taking birds with confi-dence will result in far more in the bag.

If birds settle on the trees round about I have no qualms in shooting at these sitting pigeon. The second barrel will invariably be at a sporting flying shot.

There are areas of woodland to which shooters will have access, regardless of season. Some of my favourite woods I start to visit around Christmas and continue to do so until April. In other woods the keeper will not permit pigeon shooting until after the pheasant shooting season has ended, and then only for a fairly limited period. February and early March therefore tends to be the main roost shooting period.

If you are fortunate to gain access to any woodland, either as an individual or as a member of a larger party, please do follow the basic principles so that we may all con-tinue to enjoy this wonderful sport. It is worth adding that game must be respected and that empty cartridges should be collec-ted for disposal at home.

It is always a mistake to visit favourite roosting woods too often. This is akin to over-shooting a flight pond for duck. Pigeon can equally be conditioned into seeking a safer refuge elsewhere. Follow the rules and our sport will continue to flourish.

Flighting

A form of pigeon shooting which can provide good sport is that of waylaying birds on their passage back to the roosting woods during the late afternoon and early evening. This can provide some lively flight shooting when conditions are favourable.

When a good flight is going into certain woods where access is not possible for roost shooting then I often try to intercept the line of flight when it passes over land where I do have permission to shoot. This type of pigeon shooting is best practised when the wind is really strong as the birds will then be kept at a contour-skimming height. If the conditions are calm the birds will go over out of shot. I have found March and April particularly good months for this sport.

One shoot comes to mind as typifying the sport that can be provided by evening flight shooting. It was April and two friends and I had been decoying on rape on a friend's farm in North Bedfordshire. Towards the late afternoon we returned the day's bag to the car and set off to the far side of the farm. Close to the back end of the farm lay some extensive woodland into which some huge quantities of pigeon had been flighting during each evening. There was no chance of obtaining permission to shoot in the wood but fortunately the main flight of pigeons to those woods was tending to pass over my friend's land during that period.

It was a very windy evening and my two shooting friends and myself lined a tall hedge close to the boundary. The pigeons came rushing on the wind from the extensive rape fields on my friend's and neighbouring farms. At first, the birds came in ones and twos and then in large parties. As birds were shot I presented them as decoys on the winter barley over the hedge, the idea being to attempt to divert birds over my spot since the flight was tending to pass on a fairly wide front. To a certain extent the ploy worked and one or two birds even showed an inclination to land. If a group of birds was spotted passing slightly wide then I shifted along the hedge to intercept them.

My friends and I enjoyed about an hour and a half's shooting which varied from the sporadic to lively action. I suppose you could describe this sport as a simulation to driven partridge, such was the quality of the targets we were presented with. It made a very enjoyable end to the day's sport, providing as it did a welcome change from decoying.

This type of flight shooting is always exciting and worth pursuing. However, regard must be given to the time of year and permission sought to do this in case the farmer is concerned about the disturbance which might possibly be caused to any nesting game birds.

Former Days

Pigeon shooting is primarily an opportunist activity and taking every opportunity to make a shoot is the whole essence of it. I cannot think that in the thirty years that I have spent, one way or another, in the pursuit of the wily woody, I have ever been bored.

When I was a youngster I had a single barrelled sixteen bore; indeed I still have it and would never part with it, for to hold it evokes memories of long-gone days too precious to give up. This gun is bored full choke and through it I used to push cartridges loaded with five shot. When the target was hit it was dead. I remember very few 'walkers' from this gun.

One of the pleasures I particularly remember was to go to a beautiful old mature wood close to my home and to shoot pigeon flighting during the afternoon and evening. I used to set up dead birds on the areas of flattened bracken but whether they did any good or not I cannot truly say. This I know, and that is the five or six birds which I bagged in those lovely woods during the course of an afternoon were a prize beyond worth. I realise that I appear to labour the point but I do feel very strongly that unless you have an affinity with the woods and fields, as well as a desire to hunt live quarry, then there is something very important missing from the sport. This is why, I suppose, clay pigeon shooting holds very little attraction for me.

Since I have been writing about woodlands and flight shooting I must describe a way of finding autumn sport, which can be obtained when the birds are attracted to the woods for the purpose of gleaning natural fruits rather than descending on the arable lands to glean off drilling.

My friend Doug has shooting rights to a farm in a pastoral part of Warwickshire and during the early part of the shooting season we went there to rough shoot. We noticed, however, that there was a steady passage of birds streaming to and from a large wood which has recently been incorporated into the farm. The birds which were coming to the wood were seeking acorns, of which there was a superabundance.

I hid on the margin of the wood with my decoys out on the grass field. The approaching pigeon tended to be pulled by the decoys over my position but none were attracted by them enough to land. A very nice little shoot ensued during which I fired a fair number of cartridges and picked up a very modest bag of pigeon. But I must confess that my bag of 17 pigeon cost me about 70 cartridges. Terrible wasn't it? Or was it? Here was a beautiful October day spent in a lovely environment with some truly sporting shooting. This was a day of fun and that is what it is all really about in the end. Sometimes shooters appear to get really worked up about the sport. My own philosophy is to remain very laid back – after all, this is a leisure activity and not the means of making a living. So, be inventive, be philosophical when things are not quite as successful as you would wish, but above all, *enjoy* it.

8 Memorable Moments

Stolen Shoot

Over the years, pigeon shooting has produced for me, as I know it has for many other participators, some memorable moments. These are not entirely to do with actual shooting but are incidents witnessed or experienced which have arisen from a shooting trip. These memories form part of the appeal of shooting, certainly for me at least.

One October not so long ago, my friend Mike came shooting with me on drilling and we were fortunate to put 109 birds in the bag. The following year we attempted a repeat performance during the last week of October.

Conditions had been very good and by late October farmers had completed much of the drilling and there remained few fields of fairly fresh sowing to attract the birds. I was anxious to give my friend a reasonable shoot since I had been achieving some good numbers prior to his visit and of course I had opened my big mouth and told him this. Whetting someone's appetite creates a good deal of pressure to deliver the goods.

Mike and I met up at a convenient spot in my area on the last Wednesday of the month, a warm sunny day with a blue sky and a mellow haze softening the distant horizons. I explained that it was my opinion that the best of the decoying was over and that we would probably have to do some mileage to find anything promising. Typically his reply was that he really didn't mind and that it was just great to be out of the office on such a good day.

In over eight miles of scouting we only saw two pigeons and they were disturbed, pecking grit on the roadside. I had a nagging feeling that perhaps we wouldn't find any pigeons and I tried to revive my flagging morale with the thought that I have acted out this scenario so many times in the past before finally 'clicking'.

The problem on this occasion was that, knowing my area as I do, most of the likely places which came to mind for a shoot had already been exploited or were singularly unpromising. One last chance presented itself in the form of the manager of a large farming estate which was at the time a relatively new acquisition to my shooting territory. It was only by good fortune that we actually found him in his office.

Having made some introductions, I then issued a heartfelt *cri de coeur* – did he have any idea where we might just make a shoot. The answer was reasonably encouraging. They had drilled two fields of wheat the previous week on one of their farms in a village seven miles away. I should explain that this village lay in what was to me relatively foreign territory and the land in question was totally new to me.

The manager issued us with detailed instructions of how to find the field, saying that he might be over during the afternoon as some of his men were carrying out work on land on the opposite side of the road from where we would be shooting.

We found the location easily enough and looked for the land in question. A large field of drilling presented itself exactly as described, bounded on its southern side by a stream with its usual border of eider, pussy willow and hawthorn bushes. A mass of birds were feeding with other airborne reinforcements regularly arriving to swell the throng. My euphoric, 'Yippee! we've found 'em!' turned to an 'Oh...', when close examination showed that our intended quarry was in fact an assortment of ferals, loft pigeons and stock doves with not a woody amongst them. Here was one of the largest concentrations of 'tame' pigeons I have witnessed. (Please note that stock doves are no longer on the quarry list as legitimate game. Always take care not to shoot racing pigeons as to do so may incur a hefty fine. Feral pigeons are still a legitimate target.)

My inclination I must confess in the absence of anything more worthwhile, was to go and attempt to thin out some of these 'townee' interlopers a little, but my friend drew my attention to the field beyond where a few woodies were to be seen flighting down the hedge and pitching into a hollow by the stream – not over-promising but clearly the more preferable place to be.

Gathering our gear we traipsed over the first field to the boundary hedge where we paused. Here we discussed the geography of the farm, having a slight doubt as to where our area of operations actually extended. We finally agreed that the two fields we had been directed to could only be the one we had just crossed and the one which now lay to our fore, so on we went.

In the shelter of the bushes by the stream and just below the lip of the bank we made our hides. The piece of Leaf Screen draped across the front proved almost superfluous because of the abundant natural cover provided by the profusely growing willow-herb. The decoys placed on the slope in front of us stood out well against the bare soil.

We had barely removed our guns from their slips when we had customers swinging into the decoys, coming into the westerly wind from the right. At this stage my friend was content to shoot photographs rather than pigeons but on the offer of my gun he promptly downed two very sporting birds. That little bit of action then

A hide in good natural cover makes the piece of netting almost superfluous.

prompted him to discard his camera in favour of his gun and soon we were both getting a reasonable amount of chances. The decoy pattern was becoming nicely reinforced with new recruits and a feeling bordering on smugness had crept over me that once again we had fallen on our feet.

After some time we decided that sharing a hide was inhibiting both of us so I moved 20 yards further along and this eased matters considerably. From this new position I could act as a sort of a 'sweeper' for my friend and he for me. We enjoyed some good shooting with a variety of opportunities presenting themselves – from high birds floating over to take a peek to some low fast birds twisting over the hedge into the breeze.

It was one o'clock when we fired our first shot and the action lasted until 3.45 p.m. We packed up and a count showed that we had just 60 birds between us – not a huge bag certainly but very satisfactory in the

circumstances. I should add that considering the distance to the car we had quite sufficient to carry.

When we arrived at the road a tractor was drawing out of the field opposite and I engaged the driver in conversation. He was an employee of the estate and interested in what was to him our impressive bag of pigeons. I explained to him that we had shot them on the farthest of the two fields.

'Which field did you say?' asked the tractor driver, with a tone of mischievous amusement in his voice.

'That second field over there!' said I, with some degree of suspicion.

'That's not our field, that one belongs to a man called Smith, he's a right miserable old so-and-so! You want to stay clear of him and I ain't kiddin',' said the tractor man now looking a shade more serious.

To this I countered. 'But I was told that there were two fields over here behind the village. This one here clearly has your gates,

Minimum gear, but still quite a load!

so where's the second field if it's not that one beyond?'

'Oh this isn't one field,' came the reply. 'This is two fields. We took the middle hedge out last year but we still talk about top and bottom fields. That there's where the hedge was.' He was pointing at a row of mature trees marching across the field, all that remained of a once mature hedgerow.

As we drew off my friend and I speculated as to what the possible outcome of our afternoon's 'stolen' sport might have been if Mr Smith had caught us red-handed. For instance, is ignorance an extenuating circumstance in law? Or would the case have hit the newspapers – 'Magazine Editor and shooting accomplice sentenced today, read all about it!'

When I next saw the estate manager he told me that he had come over to our location in the afternoon. Despite hearing our cannonade he could not locate our position, having no binoculars with him, but he had a feeling we were on the wrong field.

'I'm sorry about the two field business,' he added, 'but we still see this field that way.'

Needless to say, I still have my leg pulled from time to time.

A Shared Day

Although pigeon decoying could be described as a solitary sport, or at least one which only involves a couple of friends operating from one spot, it does not mean that the pigeon shooter has the countryside entirely to himself. Living in Leicestershire as I do, it is not an infrequent experience to find myself sharing an area with the hunt, which at times conveniently keeps the birds nicely moving for me. On other occasions, hounds may be working the very piece of territory I had earmarked for a likely shoot and I have been forced to seek quieter pastures.

One marvellous autumn day when hunter and shooter shared a farm without disturbance to each other happened to me not so long ago. A bean stubble on a friend's farm had been proving productive over several days and one fine Saturday afternoon I was again enjoying a steady, if not over-energetic shoot there.

The position I had chosen was very pleasant. The field sloped up and away from me and a small stream gurgled along at my back. Over the stream lay an area of small grass meadows with ancient leggy thorn hedges and stands of mature ash trees. This sheltered spot insulated me from any sound of distant traffic, an intrusion which is never very far away even in the depths of the English countryside.

The first inclination I had that other field sportsmen were around came in the form of a distant yelping, a clamouring of canine voices reminiscent perhaps of geese far off. This noise came steadily nearer when to my right a hare suddenly sprang from the brookside cover. It took a line over the hill in front of me, running perhaps at an angle of ten o'clock to my position.

Moments later I was aware of a huffing and puffing as a hare hound, in the shape of a harrier, came bursting from the brook. Nose to the earth it sniffed its way through my decoy pattern and then after giving voice, triumphantly took the same line that 'sally' had coursed a minute or two before. It was not long before three more hounds also appeared and took the same line.

It was some time before the rest of the pack, plus hare hunters, appeared milling in the meadow behind me trying desperately and noisily to seek a way through the wire fence. Some of the little hounds found their own way through fairly easily whilst others were lifted over and then the whole company, totally oblivious of the decoys, fallen birds, and me, went bounding away on very roughly, but not quite, the same line that the leading hounds had taken. I watched them depart over the skyline not at all aggrieved that they had burst upon my

Placing a dead bird in a natural, head-down position on drilling.

solitary wait and had for a time intruded upon my quiet corner. It was not long before pigeons reappeared and my little shoot resumed.

Seconds after shooting one of two absolute 'screamers' which flashed over the decoys I heard a timorous voice say, 'Excuse me please, is it all right to come through?' I looked over my shoulder and saw on the far side of the brook, attired in plus-two breeches, a voluminous sweater and incongruously large walking boots, a slightly plump lady in her mid-thirties, standing there looking slightly lost. 'Come on through by all means,' I replied, 'and by the way they went that way!'

The last of the harehunters thanked me and set off at a wearied, dragging jog. I smiled to myself and thought how absolutely first class it was that that lady should have been out there on an autumn afternoon doing her own thing in terms of healthy exercise.

I felt sure that I had seen the last of hare, hounds and hunters that afternoon but it was not so. (Whilst I recognise that a hare will run hounds round in a circle quite frequently, I have not experienced this type of incident before.) It must have been great odds against hare and hounds coming my way again that day but truth to tell, not quite an hour later the whole sequence of events happened again, almost as a re-run of the first time. The second time round though the hunt followers were much more strung out. The long-legged huntsman and the wiry whippers-in looked as if they had miles of running left in them but some of the followers were beginning to look the worse for wear, and many were interspersing short spells of jogging with longer periods of walking. I never did see the plump little lady again.

Shadows were lengthening and the best of the shooting had passed. I loaded my gear and slogged off up the bank to my car, parked up on the farm track. I had shot 42 pigeons so that was very satisfying in the circumstances, considering how the day had been made extra-interesting by the additional entertainment caused by the harriers.

I arrived at the car and found a gentleman leaning by the field gate. He expressed interest in the pigeons I had shot and we fell into conversation about field sports generally. It transpired that he was following the hounds but an injury had forced him to take a sedentary stance that afternoon. As we talked I told him that over the years I had noticed a real decline in the hare population on the farms I shoot over. He agreed and told me that on one farm they had found five dead hares. He added that a post mortem had revealed traces of slug pellets in these dead animals. Slug pellets are frequently scattered on cereals by many farmers and are easy to see by their bluish colour. This all brought to my mind the poisoned pigeons so often witnessed in the late 1950s and early 1960s, victims of the toxic cereal seed dressing then in unrestricted use. Is it not surely sad and inglorious for any quarry species to end its day thus?

The light of the late afternoon was making everything stand out in sharp relief, the rolling Leicestershire meadows and patches of woodland were painted in a way which only a clear autumn light can achieve. Across the valley the clamouring of hounds came to our ears. I hastily sought the binoculars stashed in the car. A milling throng of wagging tails in a distant meadow showed that the little hounds had at last pulled down their hare. The sound of a horn carried clearly on the wind and my acquaintance turned to me and nodded.

Appeal of Field Sports

There on a quiet afternoon two field sportsmen of different persuasions mutually saluted the appeal to be found in all hunting sports. This appeal is manifest in so many

Somewhere across this valley in Leicestershire, harriers have caught their hare and the pigeon shooter is for a while distracted from his sport.

hunting and fishing activities which are as old as man himself. These activities have endured through the centuries. They have survived the urbanisation and suburbanisation of our land and its people. Let us hope that they will long survive the moralising prophets of our 'ban everything age' and the political pressures that inevitably are to come.

It is not only fellow field sportsmen with which the pigeon shooter may find himself sharing the land. I once had a whole string of hikers, who had strayed off the footpath by several hundred yards, march straight through the decoys. Not one of them turned a blind eye to the dead birds lying round and about, except for the end two hikers, an elderly man and woman. The vestiges of conversation I managed to snatch as they lingered in their march involved an explanation from the man on

how a shoot had taken place but that he couldn't understand why no one had picked up the shot birds. He unbelievably went on to explain about beaters and lines of guns, totally confusing a formal pheasant shoot with one man's solitary pigeon shoot. The pair never did spot me and I did not show myself to them but I was certainly amused. There is a point here worth making though, as it just goes to show how confused the average citizen can be about shooting and all its various forms. It falls to all of us who love our sport to aim to be its public relations officers and promoters.

Amusing Incidents

One of the most amusing incidents that I have encountered, though, came on a warm May afternoon when out shooting with my father and a friend. My father and I had set up on opposite sides of a pea field and my friend had taken himself off to another pea field on the same farm but at least three quarters of a mile away. We had hopes of some reasonable shooting. May is often a fairly slack period for pigeon shooting. Drilling is usually finished, the rape is well grown and there may be few crops apart from peas which are really pulling birds in decoyable quantities. On the day I am describing we were occupying the only two pea fields for some distance round, hence our optimism.

It was a beautiful day, a heat haze rose off the meadows, the thorn hedges had become green ribbons criss-crossing the countryside and both oak and ash were vying with each other as to which would be first in foliage. This is a matter of interest still to some country people, remembering the old saying: 'oak before the ash, we're going to have a splash; ash before oak, we're going to have a soak.' There was certainly no hint of a soak on this spring day.

My father and I had pigeons over the decoys reasonably often. It was a day of little wind though and there was a languid feeling in the air. Nonetheless towards the latter part of the afternoon there was a real flurry of activity from the birds but this suddenly ended and nothing else happened. I was puzzled – we should have expected a little more action as this was the part of the day when pigeon activity is at its most intense at this time of the year.

It was then that I heard a murmur of voices, and poking my head out of the hide I looked down the hedge. Twenty yards away a young man had climbed through a gap and was helping his girlfriend through. The lad was carrying a blanket with him which he proceeded to spread out on the field edge. My first thought was that they were picnickers, but the absence of bag or basket quickly dispelled my belief in that.

William Shakespeare wrote, 'In the spring a young man's fancy lightly turns to thoughts of love.' It became obvious that the couple's hunger was not for food but for that other natural human acitivity which is also as old as the hunting urge. I had no intention of becoming an unwilling voyeur, however interesting the entertainment, so I climbed out of my hide and made my presence known.

It was then that the girl noticed the decoy pattern and could not contain her desire to leave, and quickly. The young man, however, showed much more interest in what I was doing. I explained what I was engaged in and asked them if they had not heard the sound of shooting. 'Oh yes,' said the boy, 'but I thought it was one of those bird-scarer things.' I smiled to myself, thinking that there are often times when that is all I am – a bird-scarer!

The young man then pointed to the far side of the field and said, 'Is it OK if we go over there?' I gently explained that my father was hidden somewhere on that side of the field and so my two amorous visitors decided to find a less crowded love nest.

Later in the day when father and I met up with our friend we found John in a lively mood. 'Hey, guess what happened to me this afternoon?' was his initial greeting. 'Don't tell me, a courting couple drifted into your decoys,' I replied. My friend looked at me as if I had finally taken leave of my senses. 'Don't be daft,' he said, and then proceeded to give a resumé of his afternoon's sport.

He had arrived at his pea field and found birds in quantity working it. The hide was quickly set up and decoys set out and then John had settled back for a spell of good shooting. He had not been thus ensconced for very long before a huge bird-like shadow loomed over him and, so he says, a glider literally clipped the hedge inches above his head and skidded to a halt on the far side of his decoys.

John said he thought for a moment that the phantom spirit of all the pigeons we had ever slain had come to take revenge. He laughingly added that his plastic decoys, which I was always in the habit of knocking, had now proved to have a far greater magnetic pigeon pulling power than anything I had employed so far.

My friend had had his afternoon's shooting interrupted quite abruptly but he certainly had gained plenty of entertainment. As I keep saying, there is more to this sport than killing pigeons.

Hawks

Writing as I do for a monthly shooting magazine, I frequently hear about other people's pigeon shooting anecdotes. The letters I receive convince me that most people engaged in this sport are having their days in the field enriched by the impact of those additional incidents which occur from time to time and are witnessed from the secrecy of a hide. Many of these anecdotes involve close encounters with birds of prey. I have heard many stories of hawks 'buzzing' the decoys or indeed even attacking decoys. I never doubt the truth of these stories for something occurred on one of my own shooting days which involved a hawk and one of my real bird decoys.

It was February and I was shooting a particularly hammered section of rape. I was using dead birds exclusively as decoys and had one or two propped up on the low, dense hedge. My hide consisted merely of a piece of net stretched across a hollow in this hedge. It was a quiet afternoon and shooting was sporadic. I became aware of a tearing sound which puzzled me as it sounded very close. I stood up and came face to face with a sparrow-hawk which was standing astride one of my dead birds on the hedge. The hawk was tearing away at the base of the pigeon's neck.

I could have reached out and touched the hawk and its 'prey', they were literally that close. The little hawk looked at me with cocked head and then resumed working on

my decoy. I watched, enthralled by this close encounter before the hawk decided that he had been intimidated enough by my presence and finally departed for a tree not thirty yards away. He lingered there for some time, appearing to be reluctant to leave an easy meal. Not so very long ago hawks were persecuted by gamekeepers to the point where they had become quite a rare sight throughout so much of our countryside. It is true to say that a more enlightened attitude happily exists today.

I believe also that the fertility of the eggs of birds of prey may have been affected by farm chemicals which was a significant contributory factor in the fall off of numbers. There is a place in our countryside for all our native wildlife, the addition of which adds life and colour to the general scene. I would expect pigeon shooters to be mindful of this and to respect all creatures which are not strictly quarry.

A Close Encounter

It was a gloomy March afternoon and the trickle of birds to the decoys had dwindled away. A creeping mist was beginning to envelop everything and I realised that the day had faded away as far as pigeon shooting was concerned. As I went to climb out of the hide, which was situated in a tall old thorn hedge bordering on a brook, something caught my eye. I froze and turned my head, cautiously. There balanced on a twig, barely two yards away, sat a kingfisher.

The little bird viewed me quizzically with its round black eye and as I watched enthralled it dropped with a plop into the little pool below our position. Within seconds the kingfisher was again on the twig and held tightly within its beak I could see a tiny squirming stickleback. Pictures of kingfishers always seem to exaggerate the size of both the bird and its prey, neither creature in real life being large.

Once more the bird dived into the brook

A pigeon shooting hide is a window on the natural world.

before it decided that the day's performance had been sufficient for my eyes and away it departed in its swooping flight, off down the brook. I watched it go, registering a flash of iridescent, electric blue before it disappeared. I was left to ponder how privileged I had been in my close encounter with this little avian fisherman, which seemed so exotically un-English, dressed in such garish plumage and appearing there on a dark and dour English afternoon.

To all pigeon shooters, both novice and experienced, I say this. The pursuit of pigeon is certainly fun and shooting at a moving, living target is always exciting. But, unless we have appreciation for all the other sights and sounds we encounter, we are missing out on so much which can be gained from this extra input to our senses,

an input which acts as seasoning to our sport.

Strange Sequence

A pigeon shooting hide is so often a peep-hole from which the natural world is seen going about its business. I once had a sequence of 'visitations' of a very coincidental nature.

One morning when decoying on rape I noticed an animal loping down the field towards me. I thought at first it was a hare but it soon became apparent that it was indeed a fox. It passed through the decoys, without giving them a second glance. Its tongue was lolling and it looked as if it had been well run. I could have bowled him over quite easily with my twelve bore considering the short distance which divided us. The farmer, with his lambs in mind, had often told me to shoot any fox which came my way. I must say though that this is something I always refrain from doing. It gives me no pleasure whatsoever to shoot a fox and since this is hunting country I am a believer in every man to his sport.

This particular morning I waited for the inevitable baying of hounds but no sound could be heard and no hunt came anywhere near me all day. The following week in a different part of my area I was more than surprised to have a similar happening occur, when a fox once again trotted close by my hide.

This is highly coincidental I am sure but what would be the odds for an incident like this occurring three times in a row? I would say those odds are pretty high, yet the following week I spotted a fox from my hide, not quite as close as on the other two occasions but nevertheless not all that far away and once again it was in the same field as myself, although on a different field from the previous two sightings.

Conclusion

In the years that I have been pigeon shooting, the basic arable farming pattern has significantly changed, and with it the pigeons' feeding behaviour has adapted accordingly, much to the frustration of many pigeon shooters. The biggest change I am referring to of course focuses upon the challenge of shooting over oil seed rape in particular, but in general it is true to say that pigeon shooters have found it becoming steadily more difficult to consistently make a reasonable sized bag of pigeon. The birds have become more wary and nowadays it just will not suffice to throw down any old decoy, regardless of its lifelike appearance.

Sometimes the impression can be portrayed to the new generation of pigeon shooters that years ago pigeon shooting was very easy, just as summers, supposedly, were always hot and every winter was filled with snow. The woodpigeon has always been a wary bird, with a well developed survival instinct, and shooting large bags still called for a degree of skill, even in those now distant halcyon days which existed before most of us were old enough to lift a gun.

Nowadays, the pigeon is pursued by more people than ever before. I suppose it is a jolly good job that it manages so often to stay one jump ahead. If every shooter became an 'expert' overnight, where would that leave the woody? Perhaps in the same state as the American Passenger Pigeon! Besides what would be the challenge in this sport if everything was too easy?

I hope those who are novice at the sport, or are young and just beginning their shooting careers, will have found the book instructional. Old hands will, hopefully, have found some useful tips – making

shell decoys is such an example. I have aspired also to convey my own philosophy towards the sport, which adheres to the proposition that pigeon shooting is fun, and is a valuable recreational outlet in which respect for the quarry species is a paramount feature. I wished, furthermore, to make my own love of the countryside and for field sports an obvious and interwoven thread within this book. I am anxious that the freedom to enjoy the countryside and its pastimes as my father and I have done should be the continuing right of my children's and their children's generations.

I have tried to be as comprehensive as possible with my handling of this fascinating sport. If you spot any gaps within the

Into battle! Pigeon shooting is fun but can be physically demanding.

text then I apologise and leave it to your own growing experience to fill them. I do sincerely hope though that pigeon shooting will continue to develop as a challenge and that no one will ever know it all.

It is Sunday afternoon as I draw this book to a conclusion and a fire is crackling in the grate. From my seat at the table I can see the wind buffeting a group of trees opposite as a flight of storm-tossed pigeon come pitching in to roost, crops bulging from their sortie on the rape. It is a scene I have experienced pleasure from on more than one previous occasion. These birds, however, are not shootable since the haven they have chosen just happens to be the grounds of a house across the road. Shooting right on my own doorstep would hold no appeal anyway, so I am content enough to sit and let the sight of these birds carry my mind off to those woods where I do have access and where, all thing being equal, future sport awaits me.

Recipes

Pigeons Normandy

1 large pigeon per person, or more if you
  want
1½ oz butter
2 medium sized dessert apples
1 medium onion
3 sticks of celery
1 tablespoon plain flour
1¼ glasses white wine
½ – ¾ pint jellied stock
Salt and pepper
1 small carton (2½ fl oz) double cream
Chopped parsley

Brown the birds slowly and carefully all
over in butter, in a flame-proof casserole.
When the birds are browned, take them out
and put in the onion, celery and apples, then
cook gently for 5–6 minutes. Remove from
the heat and stir in the flour, then add the
wine and stock. Bring to the boil, season
and put the birds back in the casserole.
Cover with grease-proof paper or foil, and
then the lid, and simmer on top of the stove
or cook in a moderate oven (pre-set 350°F,
Gas Mark 4) for 45 minutes. When the birds
are tender, take them out of the casserole
and strain the sauce, pushing as much of the
vegetable and apple mixture through the
strainer as possible. Turn into a saucepan,
adjust the seasoning and boil well. When it
has reached a syrupy consistency, add the
cream and whisk it well in. Leave to simmer
while you cut the birds in half. Arrange on
serving dish and pour some of the sauce
over.

Pigeon Pâté

1 dozen pigeons
¼ lb minced veal
1 oz white breadcrumbs
Tablespoon finely chopped onion
Clove of garlic
Basil
Grated zest of small orange
1 dessertspoon gin or brandy
Beaten egg

Cut the meat from the pigeons, and mince
or blend. Use the livers of the birds but be
sure to remove the bile duct and any yellow
staining on them. Mix with the minced
veal, breadcrumbs, finely chopped onion,
crushed garlic, a generous pinch of basil, the
zest of the orange, and the gin or brandy.
Bind with enough beaten egg to make it
moist but not sloppy. Spoon into a buttered
terrine, cover with streaky bacon, and bake
at 325°F, Gas Mark 3 in a roasting tin half-
filled with water for 45 minutes.

Julia's Shangton Woodies

Serves 4

For the sauce:	For the stock:
8 pigeons	1 pint water
3oz butter	2 carrots
3oz double cream	2 sticks of celery
3–4oz finely	Clove of garlic
chopped onion	6 parsley stalks
3fl/oz ruby port	Medium onion
1 teaspoon English	(quartered)
mustard (made)	Pint of dry basil
1oz tomato purée	Necks, giblets and
Salt and freshly	legs of birds
ground black	Small turnip
pepper	
Redcurrant jelly	

Skin the birds, remove breasts and reserve them. Make stock by simmering all stock ingredients together, spoon off scum as it rises to the top and cook until reduced to less than half. (Or, if you are feeling lazy, use a chicken stock cube as directed on the packet.) Fry the breasts quickly in the butter for about 4 minutes, reserve and keep warm. Fry the chopped onion until transparent. Add port, a dessertspoon of redcurrant jelly, mustard, a little stock and tomato purée and mix well together. Season with salt and pepper. Boil for a few minutes, then take off heat and add the cream. Shake the pan (over a low heat) to make waves in the sauce until it has thickened slightly. Keep warm.

Slice the pigeon breasts thinly, and arrange round the serving dish. Pour over the sauce and sprinkle with a little fresh parsley. For a more professional touch lightly poach julienne (very fine matchsticks) of carrot and celery in the stock, then put into sauce at the last moment. Serve with roast potatoes (these are crispiest if cooked in goose or duck dripping), and small florets of broccoli.

A Pigeon Shooter's Country Code

1. For safety's sake, be aware that others also use the countryside.
2. Leave no mess – take all litter home especially empty cartridge cases.
3. Do not use cartridges with plastic shot cups when shooting where stock may graze.
4. Do not climb through hedges.
5. Be careful not to cut valuable young trees when making natural hides.
6. Close gates.
7. Keep your dog under control.
8. Respect game and other wildlife.
9. Seek out and instantly dispatch any wounded birds.
10. Do not shoot at ground game when roost shooting.

Useful Addresses

Country Landowners Association
16 Belgrave Square
London
SW1X 8PQ

The Game Conservancy
Burgate Manor
Fordingbridge
Hampshire
SP6 1EF

British Field Sports Society
59 Kennington Road
London
SE1 7PZ

British Association for Shooting and
    Conservation
Marford Mill
Rossett
Wrexham
Clwyd

Clay Pigeon Shooting Association
107 Epping New Road
Buckhurst Hill
Essex
IG9 5TQ

Clayshooters Supplies
32 St Mary's Road
Market Harborough
Leicestershire
LE16 7DU

Shooting Developments
Valley Drive
Leslie
Fife
KY6 3BQ

East Anglian Shooting Products
The Street
Helhoughton
Norfolk
NR21 7BL

Index

Acquisition of territory   80
Aerial   50, 52, 54
Agricultural pests   12
Agriculture   15
April   46, 80, 87, 94, 106, 107
Artificial decoys   54
August   12, 80

Bale hides   68, 84
Banger guns   85
Beans   87, 91, 93
Binoculars   15, 24
Bird scarers   14
Bore   22, 107
British Association for Shooting and Conservation
   20, 125
British Field Sports Society   125

Camouflage netting   65, 106, 110
Carrying the bag   29
Cartridge loads   23
Cartridges   21–3, 77
Cartridge to kill ratio   83
Choke   22, 23
Clay Pigeon Shooting Association   125
Clay Shooters Supplies   125
Clothing   17, 32, 68
Clubs   20, 102
Country code   124
Country Landowners' Association   125
Cover   92, 103
Crop protection   20
Cropping policy   80, 120
Crops, alternative   99

December   80, 81, 96
Decoys
   artificial   37, 85
   colouring   37
   distance from hide   74, 75
   distances between   72
   frames   47, 53
   materials   37, 39
   movement   47, 52, 90
   pattern   47, 54, 71, 75, 85
   posture   37, 72
   real birds   39, 47, 54, 72, 85
   setting out   37, 71
   shell   37, 55

venues   99
Decoying on rape   84
Disposal of bag   77
Dogs
   control   85
   function   33
   ideal breed   35
   training   35
Drilling   20, 54, 87, 109

East Anglian Percher   43
East Anglian Shooting Products   41, 125
Easter   19, 89
Equipment   21

Farmers   12, 14, 16
Farms   27, 80
February   46, 80, 106
Feral pigeons   110
Field sports, appeal   114, 120
Flappers   48
Flexicoys   39
Flight lines   81, 102
Flighting   107
Flutterers   90
Formaldehyde   57
Freezing birds   79

Game carriers   29, 83, 93
Game Conservancy   125
Game dealers   78
Gamekeeper   18
Grass screen   66
Ground game   102
Gun security   24
Gundogs   33
Guns   21–6
Gunsmith   22

Hawks   117
Head covering   33
Hearing damage   29, 31
Hearing protection   29
Hides
   construction   27, 65
   discipline in   67
   siting   46, 68, 70
   use of natural foliage   65–6

January   18, 80
July   12, 80
June   12, 99

Laid cereals   43, 86, 95
Litter   16, 17, 124
Lofting decoys   39, 43, 46, 106
Lofting frames   43, 46, 94–5

March   80, 106, 117
Marksmanship   24, 34
May   80, 83, 115
Memorable moments   109

Netting   27–9, 65, 75, 106

October   96, 108, 109
Oil seed rape   43, 80, 90
Organised trips   102
Overhead cover   67, 92

Peas   87, 94, 116
Pest control   11, 78
Permission to shoot   14, 16, 80
Pigeon shooting, sale   15
Pigeons
   disposal   77
   favoured positions   81, 83, 98
Populations   15

Recipes   122
Reconnaissance and observation   15, 27, 68, 70
Regional differences   15
Regional names   12

Retrieval   34–5
Richardson, Maurice   41, 43, 47, 66, 74
Richardson Rocker   41, 43, 48, 57
Roost shooting   18, 75, 100
Rough shooting   75, 80
Rules   17

Safety   68, 102, 124
Seasonal differences   84
Seating   32
Seeking permission   16
Selling pigeons   77
September   94, 96
Shell decoys
   use   54, 94
   made from real birds   54, 85
Shooting Developments   125
Shooting from hides   67, 77
Shooting position   75
Shot cups, plastic   23, 24
Shot patterns   23, 106
Snow   19, 100
Sportsmanship   11, 78
Stock doves   110
Storry, John   41
Stubble   86, 95
Swathe-rowing   85

Territory, acquisition   15
Treatment of shot birds   78

Weather conditions   80, 81, 84, 89, 93, 100
Wind   72, 74, 81, 89, 92, 99, 100
Wounded birds, dispatch   24